HEALTHY BOUNDARIES RESET

TRUST GOD'S DESIGN TO STOP PEOPLE-PLEASING,
OVERCOME CODEPENDENCY, AND LOVE WITHOUT
LOSING YOURSELF

PROMISE PATH PRESS

7-Day Healthy Boundaries Reset Companion

A practical companion to support your 7-day reset and help you apply healthy boundaries in real life.

As you begin Healthy Boundaries Reset, this companion toolkit is here to help you slow down and practice what you're learning. One calm, grounded step at a time.

The goal isn't perfection.
It's awareness, clarity, and small, sustainable changes that protect your peace.

Inside the Companion Toolkit, you'll find:

- **Simple** daily practices to support your 7-day reset
- **Clear** scripts to help you respond without over-explaining
- **Gentle** reminders to check your capacity before saying yes
- **Faith-rooted** encouragement to pause, check your capacity, and choose wisely

These resources are meant to be used alongside the book whenever you need extra support or a reset.

To access your companion toolkit, scan the QR code below or visit:

https://tinyurl.com/HealthyBoundariesReset

(No sign-up required. You can return to this resource anytime.)

Scan me

---

*"Come to Me, all you who are weary and burdened, and
I will give you rest."*
— Matthew 11:28

CONTENTS

BEFORE YOU BEGIN

Before you dive in, I want you to unclench your jaw.

Drop your shoulders away from your ears.

Take a breath. In through your nose, out through your mouth.

You don't need to brace yourself to become a "tougher" person. You don't need to prepare for a fight. You don't even need to believe you're ready to say "No" yet. Just breathe, and be willing to be curious.

This isn't a book about building walls or cutting people off. It is a conversation, a gentle one, about remembering that you are a person, not a resource.

I don't know your story yet, but I do know this: if you're reading these words, you are tired. You have loved through exhaustion, given until you were empty, and kept showing up even when your soul was asking for a break. That takes a massive amount of love.

The world calls it "being nice."

I call it "forgetting your own address."

You were designed for a life of stewardship, not slavery. The problem isn't that you are generous; it's that you've been trying to pour from a cup that has a hole in the bottom.

That's why this book exists: not to make you hard, but to make you whole. To show you that setting a boundary isn't an act of war; it's an act of peace. It is how you protect the love you have so it doesn't turn into resentment.

And faith plays a huge role in this. For me, faith has always been the reminder that God is the Savior, not me. It reminds me that the world will keep spinning even if I take a nap.

So before we begin, I want you to know: You are allowed to rest. You are allowed to have limits. You are allowed to be human.

Take one more deep breath.

You've already taken your first step toward freedom.

Read This First

If you've picked up this book, I want you to know something from the start: **You are not "mean" for needing space.**

You are not "selfish" for needing sleep. And you are not a "bad Christian" for admitting that you cannot do everything.

If you have ever found yourself saying "Yes" with a smile while your stomach screamed "No," or if you've ever felt the heavy, wet-concrete dread of disappointing someone you love, you are in the right place.

This book is a reset. Not a crash course in being aggressive. Not a manual on how to be difficult. A reset. For your conscience. For your calendar. For the way you relate to the people who rely on you.

Together, we're going to walk through why you feel responsible for everyone else's feelings, why "being nice" has become an idol, and what it actually looks like to love people without losing yourself.

We're going to talk about the "Resentful Yes," the "Vulnerability Hangover," and why Jesus walked away from needy crowds to go pray.

We will talk about God, not as a Taskmaster tallying your service hours, but as a Gardener who created days and nights because He knew His creation needed rhythm.

You won't be scolded here. You won't be told to just "toughen up." You'll be guided, grounded, and reminded over and over again: **Your "No" protects your "Yes."**

This isn't about stopping your love. It's about making your love sustainable.

Let's reset, together.

HOW TO USE THIS BOOK

First things first: there's no "right way" to use this book. You don't need to implement every boundary by Tuesday. Think of this less like a rulebook and more like a toolkit. You grab the hammer when you need to build a fence, and you grab the chair when you need to sit down.

Here's what will help you get the most out of it:

- **Read at your own pace.** Some chapters (like the ones on family guilt) might hit hard; take your time. Others might be a gentle reminder. Both are wins.
- **Use the Scripts.** You will find specific words to say in almost every chapter (and in the Appendix). Don't just read them; say them out loud. Your voice needs to practice the sound of your own limits.
- **Notice the Call-Outs:**
    - **THE GATEKEEPER'S TRUTH:** These are theological anchors to replace the lies of "niceness."
    - **THE BOUNDARY BUILDER:** These are practical audits and action steps to help you move from theory to reality.

- **Expect the "Wobble."** When you start setting boundaries, it feels scary. You will feel guilty. That is normal. Come back to **Chapter 10** whenever you have a "Vulnerability Hangover."

Above all, give yourself permission to be messy. You are unlearning a lifetime of people-pleasing. It's okay if your voice shakes the first time you say no.

Just say it anyway.

WHY FAITH BELONGS
IN THIS CONVERSATION

You might wonder why a book about boundaries discusses God. Shouldn't this be all about assertiveness training and psychology?

We'll cover the psychology. But here's the thing:

Your struggle with boundaries isn't just a personality quirk. It is often a theological confusion.

Many of us were raised with a version of faith that equated "holiness" with "having no needs." We learned that to be like Jesus meant to be endlessly available, constantly self-sacrificing, and never inconvenient. We learned that "Love your neighbor" meant "Fix your neighbor."

But when we look at Scripture, we see a God of boundaries.

In Genesis 1, the very first thing God did to bring life out of chaos was to draw lines. He separated light from darkness. He separated sea from land. He created order.

Throughout the Gospels, we see Jesus, the embodiment of Love, setting limits. He withdrew to the wilderness. He said no to demands. He disappointed people by staying true to His mission.

If we try to build boundaries without faith, we just end up feeling guilty or arrogant. But when we bring God into it, we realize that boundaries are actually **stewardship**.

God gave you a life, a body, a heart, and a specific amount of energy. He expects you to steward those resources, not squander them to keep everyone happy.

That's why faith belongs here. Because your "No" isn't a rejection of people; it is an act of worship to the God who made you finite. It is an admission that He is God, and you are not.

This isn't about using the Bible to wall people out. It's about discovering that the most loving thing you can do for the world is to offer it a version of you that isn't burnt out, resentful, or hiding.

You were made to love. And you were made to last.

THE BLUEPRINT SUBTITLE:
THE ARCHITECTURE OF
A SUSTAINABLE LIFE

I want to start by asking you a question, and I want you to be honest with me. Not "church honest," where you smile and say you're blessed, but *real* honest, the kind of honest you are at 2:00 AM when you're staring at the ceiling.

How does your stomach feel right now?

Does it feel light? Does it feel settled? Or does it feel like someone just poured a bag of wet concrete into your gut?

I ask because I know that feeling. It is the distinct, heavy, sinking sensation of what I call "The Resentful Yes." You know the moment I'm talking about. It happens when someone asks you for something, a favor, a volunteer shift, a loan, a listening ear, and every fiber of your being screams, *"No, please, not today, I'm empty."*

But then, the Override Switch flips. Your mouth opens, a smile you don't feel plasters itself onto your face, and you hear your own voice say, *"I'd love to!"*

And immediately, you feel sick.

You walk away from that interaction not feeling generous but feeling robbed. You feel that familiar cocktail of guilt, dread, and exhaustion settling into your bones. You aren't just tired because you're busy; you are tired because you are leaking. You are leaking energy, time, and emotional capacity into places you never actually agreed to pour into, at least, not with your whole heart.

If you are holding this book, I am guessing you are exhausted. Not the kind of exhaustion that a nap can fix, but the kind of deep, soul-level fatigue that comes from years of over-functioning. You are the one who fixes. You are the one who shows up. You are the safety net for your family, the emotional regulator for your spouse, the shock absorber for your workplace, and the most reliable volunteer at your church. You are the person everyone else counts on to keep the world from falling apart.

But somewhere along the way, you realized that while you were busy holding everyone else's world together, your own world started to crumble.

You might be reading this thinking, *"But isn't that what love is? Isn't love about sacrifice? Isn't it about laying down my life?"* We have absorbed a version of faith that equates "holiness" with having no needs. We have convinced ourselves that having limits is a sin, and that if we were *really* spiritual, we would be infinite. We would be able to give and give and give without ever needing to stop and refill.

But friend, I need to tell you a hard truth: You are not infinite. You are human. And trying to live without limits isn't an act of faith; it is an act of rebellion against your own creation.

From Survival to Sustainability

We are going to do deep work in these pages. We are going to dismantle the scripts that told you "No" was a bad word. But before we build the new structure, we have to look at the foundation we've already laid.

If you read my previous book, *Anxious Attachment Reset*, you remember we touched on boundaries in Chapter 9. We talked about them as "emergency brakes", a way to stop the spiral of panic and keep you safe. That was the 101 level: learning that it's okay to say no.

But this book is the Master Class. We aren't just trying to stop the panic anymore; we are trying to build a life. We are moving beyond the basic "No" and into the complex, beautiful architecture of a life that can sustain long-term love without burnout. If Book 1 was about survival, this book is about sustainability. It's time to stop just "setting" boundaries and start living within them.

In Book 1, we focused on finding safety in *connection*. We learned how to reach out, how to trust that love wouldn't leave, and how to soothe the panic of abandonment. But here is the paradox of secure attachment: You cannot have a safe connection without a safe separation.

If you don't know where you end and another person begins, that isn't intimacy. That is enmeshment. And enmeshment is exhausting. It means their bad mood becomes your bad mood. Their crisis becomes your emergency. Their disappointment becomes your failure. You become a thermometer, constantly adjusting your internal temperature to match the room, rather than a thermostat set by God.

This book is about finding safety in *separation*. It is about learning that you can step back and still be loved. It is about realizing that "No" is not a rejection of the other person; it is a stewardship of the self God gave you to manage.

The Theology of Order

I know the word "separation" can sound scary to the anxious heart. It sounds like distance. It sounds like the very thing we spent the last book trying to heal from! But I want to take you back to the very beginning of the story, before trauma, before anxiety, before the fall. I want to take you to Genesis 1.

When you look at the creation narrative, what is the very first thing God does? The earth was "formless and empty," and chaos (or *tohu wa-*

bohu in Hebrew) was everywhere. God didn't just pour more love into the chaos. He didn't just hug the chaos.

He drew lines.

He separated. He separated the light from the darkness. He separated the water from the dry land. He separated the day from the night. God is a God of order, not chaos. He created boundaries so that life could flourish.

Think about it: God did not look at the ocean and say, *"I don't want to be mean to the water, so I'll just let it go wherever it wants."* No. He set a boundary. He said to the sea, *"This far you may come and no farther"* (Job 38:11).

Why? Was He rejecting the water? No. He was creating a space where dry land could exist. Without that boundary, there would be no trees, no animals, no gardens, no us. Life requires structure. Life *requires* separation.

Your life is a garden entrusted to you by God. It has soil (your heart), resources (your energy), and fruit (your love). But if that garden has no fences, if your neighbor can drive their truck through your flowerbeds, if stray dogs can dig up your vegetables, if anyone can dump their trash on your lawn, you do not have a garden. You have a vacant lot. You have *tohu wa-bohu*.

Boundaries are simply the property lines that define where your garden begins and ends. They define what you are responsible *for* and what you are responsible *to*. When we refuse to set boundaries because we are afraid of being "mean" or "unchristian," we are actually refusing to do the work of a gardener. We are letting the chaos back in.

God wants more for you than a life of trampled soil and stolen fruit. He wants you to have a harvest. And to have a harvest, you need a fence.

The Gate vs. The Wall

Now, when I say "fence," I know what image might pop into your head. You might picture a ten-foot concrete wall topped with razor wire. You might picture a fortress where you sit alone, safe but isolated.

This is the binary thinking that keeps us stuck. We think our only two options are:

1. **The Doormat**: No walls, everyone walks all over us, but we are "connected" (and resentful).
2. **The Fortress**: Giant walls, no one gets in, we are safe (but lonely).

But there is a third option. It is the biblical option. It is the sustainable option.

We are not building walls to shut people out; we are building fences with *gates*.

A wall says, "Go away, I don't want you." A gate says, "I control access to this space". A wall is static; it separates forever. A gate is dynamic; it opens and closes based on wisdom, safety, and capacity.

When you install a gate, you aren't cutting people off. You are simply installing a latch. You are giving yourself the ability to decide who comes in, when they come in, and how long they stay.

Imagine your life is a house. If you take the front door off the hinges and let anyone walk in at 3:00 AM, track mud on the carpet, and eat all the food in your fridge, you aren't being "hospitable." You are being unsafe. You are letting your home become a public thoroughfare. And eventually, your house will be wrecked. You won't have anything left to give to the people you actually *want* to invite in.

But if you have a door with a lock, you can open it wide when a friend comes over. You can welcome them in with joy because you know your space is safe. You can offer them tea and presence because you aren't exhausted from chasing out intruders all night.

The person with the strongest boundaries is often the most loving person in the room. Why? Because they are not resentful. When you know you have a gate, when you know you can close it if you need to, you feel safe enough to leave it open when you want to.

This book is about building that gate.

A New Definition of Love

This journey will require us to redefine some of our most sacred words. We are going to have to redefine "nice." We are going to have to redefine "selfish." And most importantly, we are going to have to redefine "love."

For too long, we have believed that love means "availability." We have believed that to be a good Christian, a good mother, a good spouse, or a good friend, we must be endlessly accessible. We have treated our lives like a 24-hour convenience store, keeping the "Open" sign buzzing neon red even when the shelves are empty, and the clerk is asleep on the counter.

But convenience store love is cheap. It's transactional. And it's exhausting.

We are going for something deeper. We are going for *Wholehearted Love*. And Wholehearted Love requires a "No."

Think about it: If you cannot say "No," your "Yes" means nothing. If you say "Yes" to everything because you are afraid, that isn't a gift; it's a ransom payment. You are paying for your safety with your compliance. But when you have the freedom to say, "I can't do that," then your "I would love to" becomes gold. It becomes a voluntary offering.

In this book, we are going to learn how to give voluntary offerings again.

We are going to look at the "Resentful Yes" and learn how to catch it before it leaves our mouths. We are going to look at the guilt that hits you like a truck the moment you set a limit, and we are going to learn how to distinguish between the conviction of the Holy Spirit and the condemnation of old conditioning.

We are going to talk about family dynamics, friendships that drain you, and workplaces that demand your soul. We are going to learn practical scripts, actual words you can say when your brain freezes up, so that you don't have to rely on willpower in the moment of pressure.

And we are going to do all of this with the understanding that God is with us. He is not tapping His foot, waiting for you to get it together. He is the Good Shepherd who leads you beside *still* waters, not frantic ones. He is the One who withdrew to the mountains to pray when the crowds were pressing in. If Jesus, the Savior of the world, needed boundaries to sustain His ministry, who are we to think we don't?

You Are Ready

If you are feeling nervous right now, that is okay. The part of you that has survived by being "the easy one" is probably trembling a little. It's whispering, *"But if I stop doing everything, will they still love me? If I close the gate, will anyone knock?"*

That fear is real. But it is a liar.

You are loved not for what you do, but for who you are. You are loved not for your utility, but for your existence. And the people who truly love you? They want *you*. They don't want the exhausted, resentful shell of you. They want the vibrant, rested, wholehearted you.

They want the version of you that exists behind the gate.

So, take a deep breath. You don't have to build the whole fence today. You don't have to fire everyone in your life tomorrow. We are going to do this one picket, one latch, one "No," and one honest "Yes" at a time.

You have survived the chaos. Now, let's build the garden.

Let's reset.

1

WHY BOUNDARIES FEEL UNLOVING (BUT AREN'T)

I f I asked you to define "love," you'd probably use words like patient, kind, selfless, and sacrificial. You might think of the famous passage in 1 Corinthians 13, or maybe a picture of a mother giving her last crust of bread to her child. You might think of Jesus washing the disciples' feet, dirty, humble, and endlessly available.

You probably wouldn't think of the word "No."

For most of us, especially those of us raised in faith communities or families that prized harmony above all else, we were handed a script for love that looked a lot like erasure. We learned early on that being a loving person meant being an available person. It meant being the one who brings the casserole even when you have the flu. It meant being the one who stays on the phone for an hour listening to a friend vent, even when you're on a deadline. It meant being the one who always says, "Sure, I can do that!" even when your soul is sinking, whispering, *Please, absolutely not.*

We learned that having needs was "high maintenance" and having limits was "selfish." So, we got really good at the "Yes." We collected "Yeses" like gold stars.

"Yes, I can lead that committee."

"Yes, you can crash on my couch for three weeks."

"Yes, it's totally fine that you're late again."

If you read my previous book, *Anxious Attachment Reset*, you remember we touched on boundaries in Chapter 9. We talked about them as "emergency brakes", a way to stop the spiral of panic and keep you safe. That was the 101 level: learning that it's okay to say no.

But this book is the Master Class. We aren't just trying to stop the panic anymore; we are trying to build a life. We are moving beyond the basic "No" and into the complex, beautiful architecture of a life that can sustain long-term love without burnout. If Book 1 was about survival, this book is about sustainability. It's time to stop just "setting" boundaries and start living within them.

Because if you are reading this book, I'm guessing you've discovered the dirty little secret about all those "Yeses" you've been collecting.

They aren't free. They cost you *you*. And eventually, the bill comes due.

THE ANATOMY OF THE "RESENTFUL YES"

Let's talk about a phenomenon I call the "Resentful Yes." You know this feeling intimately, even if you've never named it. It happens when your mouth says, "I'd love to!" while your stomach feels like someone just poured wet concrete into it.

I watched a good friend of mine, let's call her Hannah, live this out in real-time. Hannah is the kind of friend everyone wants. She's dependable, hilarious, and deeply empathetic. She is the person you call when your tire blows out or your heart gets broken. But because she is so good at showing up, people have forgotten that she might need to show up for herself, too.

One Tuesday, her sister called. It was a frantic, high-speed request: could Hannah babysit her three kids for the weekend, last-minute, so the sister could go on a getaway with her husband?

Now, context matters here. Hannah had just come off a month of sixty-hour work weeks. She was physically exhausted. Her fridge was empty, her laundry was a mountain, and she had planned to spend the weekend sleeping and staring at a wall in glorious silence. Her body was practically begging for rest.

But when she heard her sister's voice, stressed, hopeful, needing a break, Hannah's programming kicked in.

Have you ever tried to say "No," but your voice literally wouldn't work? You wanted to decline the request, but your head started nodding "Yes" like a bobblehead doll before you even gave it permission?

That is not a lack of willpower; that is the **Appeasement Reflex**. Your nervous system perceives the other person's potential disappointment as a physical threat. To protect you, it bypasses your logical brain entirely and hijacks your vocal cords to offer the "Yes" that ensures immediate safety. You aren't lying; you are surviving.

"Of course!" Hannah chirped, her voice jumping up an octave. "Go have fun! I've got the kids. Don't worry about a thing."

She hung up the phone, and the atmosphere in her body shifted instantly. It wasn't the frantic, racing heartbeat of panic; it was the heavy, sinking sensation of dread. Her shoulders instinctively slumped, and she felt the heavy weight of the Fawn response, her body's desperate attempt to reconnect by becoming small and compliant.

Then, the dread turned into anger. *Does she have any idea how tired I am? Why does she always ask me? She knows I can't say no.*

By the time Friday rolled around, Hannah wasn't a loving aunt. She was a simmering volcano of resentment. When the kids spilled juice, she snapped at them. When her sister texted for an update, Hannah sent back a curt, passive-aggressive reply. She spent the entire weekend feeling used, unappreciated, and bitter.

Here is the hard truth we need to swallow: Hannah didn't love her sister that weekend. **Hannah lied to her.**

She served her sister, yes. She helped her sister, sure. But she was not loving her. She was silently resenting her. She was building a ledger of debt that her sister didn't even know she was accruing.

THE WORKPLACE MARTYR

This phenomenon isn't limited to families, and it certainly isn't limited to women. It happens just as often in the office, though we usually disguise it as "being a team player."

Take Mark, for example. Mark is a mid-level manager at a logistics company and a devout Christian. He takes the command to be "salt and light" in his workplace very seriously. To Mark, that means being the most helpful, most available guy in the building.

If a colleague drops the ball on a report, Mark quietly fixes it late at night so they don't get in trouble. If his boss sets an unrealistic deadline, Mark says, "We'll get it done," and then works through the weekend while the rest of the team is at the beach. He believes that by absorbing the stress of the office, he is witnessing to Christ's sacrificial love.

But after two years of this, Mark wasn't glowing with the light of Christ. He was burnt out, cynical, and critical.

He sat in my office one day and confessed, "I resent everyone I work with. I look at my coworker, Dave, leaving at 5:00 PM every day while I'm still there until 7:00, and I just want to scream. I'm doing his job and mine. But if I stop, the team fails. I feel like I'm trapped."

Here is what Mark missed: By constantly saving Dave from the consequences of his own laziness, Mark wasn't loving Dave. He was enabling him. And worse, he was presenting a false reality.

Because Mark never set a boundary, Dave never learned to improve. Dave assumed everything was fine because the work always magically got done. Mark thought he was being a "Servant Leader," but he was actually just being a "Secret Martyr." And the cost? When Mark got home at 7:30 PM, exhausted and bitter, he had nothing left for his wife, Rachel, and their kids. He was giving his best energy to a coworker who didn't appreciate it and giving his leftovers to the people he loved most.

This is the core conflict of this book: A "Yes" born from fear, or a "Yes" born from a need to be the hero, is not love. **It's a lie.**

When we say yes but mean no, we are introducing dishonesty into our relationships. We are presenting a false version of ourselves, the "easy, low-maintenance, super-human" version, and hiding the real, tired, limited version. We think we are keeping the peace, but we are actually building a wall of hidden frustration that will eventually crumble.

Real love requires honesty. And sometimes, the most honest thing you can say is, "I love you, but I can't do that."

THE "SELFISH" TRAP (AND WHAT JESUS HAS TO SAY ABOUT IT)

Now, let's tackle the biggest hurdle right out of the gate: The God Card.

I can hear the objection because I've whispered it to myself a thousand times, usually at 3:00 AM while worrying about an email I sent: *But aren't Christians supposed to be self-sacrificing? Isn't it holy to put others first? If I set boundaries, am I just being a selfish modern person who reads too much self-help?*

It's a fair question. We serve a God who gave everything. We are called to pick up our cross. So, where do boundaries fit into a faith that is defined by sacrifice?

Let's look at the life of Jesus. You know, the literal definition of Love incarnate.

If anyone had a reason to say "Yes" to everyone, it was Jesus. He could heal the sick, raise the dead, and fix broken hearts. Every moment He spent sleeping was a moment He wasn't healing someone. Every time He walked away from a crowd, He was leaving needy people behind. The stakes were infinite.

And yet... He walked away. A lot.

He set boundaries with crowds: "But Jesus often withdrew to lonely places and prayed." (Luke 5:16). He didn't heal everyone in Judea. He left towns where people were still sick because He needed to go elsewhere. He didn't let the needs of the crowd dictate His schedule.

He set boundaries with His family: When His mother and brothers came to collect Him because they thought He was working too hard, He didn't drop everything to appease them. He stayed focused on what God had called Him to do.

Jesus did not have a "savior complex"; He *was* the Savior, and even He respected the limits of His humanity while He walked on earth. If the Son of God often withdrew to rest, pray, and reset, who are we to think we don't need to?

THE STEWARDSHIP OF TRUTH

This brings us to a more advanced definition of boundaries. We often think of boundaries as defense, but I want you to think of them as **Stewardship**.

In *Anxious Attachment Reset*, we defined boundaries as a way to stay safe. But now, we're going deeper. In this book, we define boundaries as a form of truth-telling. A relationship built on your exhaustion isn't love; it's a transaction. We are moving from "boundaries as self-defense" to "boundaries as stewardship", the holy work of managing the limited resources God gave you.

True stewardship is recognizing that you are a finite resource. If you are a car, God needs you to drive. But if you never stop for gas because you think stopping is "selfish," you aren't going to drive very far. You're going to break down on the side of the road. And a broken-down car can't help anyone.

When you set a boundary, you aren't being selfish. You are refueling. You are ensuring that when you do say yes, you are bringing your full, loving, cheerful self to the table, not the resentful, exhausted shell of yourself. God loves a cheerful giver, not a miserable, burnt-out one.

THE VOLUNTEER TRAP: WHEN "SERVICE" BECOMES SLAVERY

This pattern doesn't just happen with families and work. It happens in our communities, and especially in our churches.

I know a woman named Lisa who is the backbone of her church. If the doors are open, Lisa is there. She runs the nursery rotation, she organizes the meal trains, and she is the first one to arrive for setup and the last one to leave after cleanup.

Everyone loves Lisa. They call her a "servant heart." They say, "I don't know what we'd do without her."

But if you catch Lisa in the parking lot on a Tuesday, she looks gray. She hasn't sat through a full sermon in three years because someone is always pulling her aside to fix a problem. She dreads checking her email because she knows it will be another request she feels she can't refuse.

Lisa isn't serving out of overflow anymore. She is serving out of oblig-ation. She is serving out of the fear that if she stops, everything will fall apart, and people will be disappointed in her.

One day, Lisa finally hit a wall. She told the pastor she needed to step down from the nursery coordination. It was terrifying for her. She expected the roof to cave in.

The pastor was surprised, but he said, "Okay. We'll figure it out."

And you know what happened? The church didn't close. The babies were still cared for. Another couple stepped up, people who had been waiting in the wings but never volunteered because "Lisa always had it covered."

By over-functioning, Lisa had unintentionally prevented others from stepping into their own roles. Her "Yes" was blocking someone else's opportunity to serve.

When she finally set a boundary, she didn't just get her Sunday mornings back. She got her joy back. And six months later, when she signed up to greet at the front door once a month, she did it with a genuine smile, not a fake one.

WHY WE THINK BOUNDARIES ARE "MEAN"

If the "Resentful Yes" feels so terrible, and if Jesus modeled limits, why do we still feel so guilty? Why does saying "No" feel like we just kicked a puppy?

Because for the anxious attachment heart (and the people-pleasing heart), the alternative feels dangerous. We believe a very specific lie: Boundaries = Rejection.

We worry that if we set a limit, we are telling the other person, "I don't care about you."

If I say "No" to the volunteer slot, I'm saying I don't care about the mission.

If I tell my mom I can't talk every day, I'm saying I don't love her.

We conflate access with affection. We think that to love someone, we must grant them unlimited access to our time, energy, and emotions.

But let's look at this through a different lens. Think of a house.

We used to fear walls because they felt like rejection. But now we realize we aren't building fortress walls to keep people out; we are building structural walls to keep the roof from collapsing on our heads. A house without walls isn't "open" and "welcoming"; it is a pile of rubble waiting to happen.

Your boundaries are the structural supports of your relationships. They hold the roof up. They ensure that the relationship remains sustainable, safe, and functional. Without them, the weight of everyone's needs will eventually crush the relationship flat.

When you put up a wall, you aren't saying, "Stay away." You are saying, "I value this house enough to make sure it doesn't fall down." You are creating a structure where love can actually live for the long haul.

THE ART OF THE PAUSE: YOUR FIRST TOOL

So, how do we start? Do we have to go home today and fire everyone? Do we have to quit all our committees and stop answering the phone?

No. That's crash-dieting, and it never works.

We start with one simple tool. It is the most powerful weapon in your boundary arsenal, and it costs nothing.

It is **The Pause**.

The "Resentful Yes" thrives on speed. It happens when someone asks you for something, and your brain goes into that bobblehead mode. You feel the pressure of their eyes on you, or the silence on the phone, and you blurt out "Yes" just to relieve the tension.

Your goal for this chapter is not to learn to say "No." It is simply to stop saying "Yes" immediately.

We need to buy your brain some time to catch up with your mouth. We need to create a gap between the Request and your Response.

Here are three scripts you can use this week. Memorize them. Write them on a sticky note. Tattoo them on your arm if you have to.

Script 1: The "Let Me Check"

"That sounds like such a great opportunity. I need to check my capacity/calendar before I commit. I'll get back to you by [Day]."

Script 2: The "Spouse/Prayer" Buffer

"I've made a promise to [my spouse/myself] not to say yes to anything new right away. I'm going to take a day to think about this."

Script 3: The "Not Right Now"

"I can't give you an answer right this second, but I can let you know by tomorrow."

Do you see what these scripts do? They don't say "No" (which is scary). They just press the pause button. They give you permission to walk away, check in with your body (is your stomach heavy?), check in with your reality (are you already exhausted?), and then decide.

Closing the Loop: What Happens After the Pause?

Okay, so you've used the Pause. You told your sister you'd "check your calendar." You hung up the phone. You checked in with yourself and realized, *Nope. I cannot babysit this weekend without falling apart.*

Now comes the part that gives most people hives: The Follow-Up.

The Pause is only helpful if you actually close the loop. If you just leave them hanging, you're not setting a boundary; you're ghosting, which creates anxiety for everyone.

But how do you deliver the "No" without sounding mean?

The trick is to be clear, kind, and brief. We often fall into the trap of JADE: Justify, Argue, Defend, Explain. We feel like a simple "No" isn't enough, so we invent a lie ("I think I might be coming down with a cold") or we over-explain ("I would, but my washing machine broke and I have to wait for the repair guy...").

You do not need to provide a legal defense for your limits.

Here is the "Sandwich Method" for closing the loop. You sandwich the "No" between two slices of kindness.

Slice 1 (Affirmation): "I love that you asked me, and I hope you guys have a great time..."

The Meat (The Limit): "...but I looked at my schedule, and I'm not going to be able to take the kids this weekend."

Slice 2 (Well Wishes): "I'm cheering you on to find someone else!"

Notice what is missing? I didn't say why. I didn't say, "Because I'm tired." I just said I wasn't able to. That is enough.

If you decide to say yes after the pause, great! That is an intentional Yes. If you decide to say no, you can do it via text or email later, when the pressure is off.

A New Definition of Love: The Gatekeeper's Truth

So, here is our starting line. We are going to reset our definition of what it means to be a loving person.

Old Definition: Love means saying yes, having no needs, and keeping everyone else happy at my own expense.

New Definition: Love means showing up honestly. It means respecting myself enough to have limits and respecting you enough to be truthful with you.

We are holding on to **The Gatekeeper's Truth**: You cannot give what you do not possess.

In this book, we aren't just going to learn how to set limits. We are going to learn how to love better. We are going to build relationships that are real, not just polite. We are going to trade the "Resentful Yes" for the "Honest No" and the "Wholehearted Yes."

It's scary. It goes against every "nice girl" or "good guy" instinct you have. But it is the only path to a love that lasts.

You are not failing at love by needing boundaries. You are learning how to make your love sustainable.

The Boundary Builder: A Reflection

Before we move to Chapter 2, I want you to be honest with yourself. You don't have to change anything today; just notice. Awareness is always the first step.

Take a pen, yes, a real one, and answer these three questions. Don't overthink it.

1. Where in my life am I giving a "Resentful Yes"? (Is it a specific relationship? A volunteer role? A coworker who takes advantage of you? A family expectation?)
2. What does my body feel like when I say yes to that thing? (Heavy? Numb? Do my shoulders slump? Do I feel a sense of dread or "wet concrete" in my stomach?)
3. What am I afraid would happen if I said "No" or set a limit there? (Be specific: "They would get mad," "I would feel guilty," "They wouldn't love me anymore," "God would be disappointed.")

Write it down. Getting the fear out of your head and onto paper is the first step in taking away its power.

You are doing good work. Let's keep going.

2

WHEN GUILT MASQUERADES
AS CONVICTION

G uilt is persuasive.

It speaks with urgency. It sounds authoritative. It feels heavy, like a wet wool blanket draped over your shoulders the moment you even think about saying "no."

If you are a person of faith, guilt often comes dressed up in spiritual language. It doesn't just say, "You're disappointing them." It says, "You're being un-Christlike." It whispers, "If you were really a servant, you wouldn't mind this." It tells you that your exhaustion is a sign of holiness, and your desire for rest is a sign of weakness.

You have probably noticed the pattern. You set a boundary, maybe you told your mom you couldn't host Thanksgiving this year, or you told a friend you couldn't loan them money again. You did it clearly. You did it kindly. You followed the scripts we talked about in the last chapter.

But the moment the words left your mouth, you didn't feel the "peace that passes understanding." You felt sick.

The atmosphere in your body shifted. It wasn't the frantic, racing heartbeat of panic; it was the heavy, sinking sensation of dread. It felt as if someone had poured wet concrete into your stomach. Your shoulders instinctively slumped, and you felt a sudden, desperate urge to fix the silence, to smile, to apologize, to over-explain, just to lift the heaviness in the room.

In that moment, it is very easy to misinterpret what your body is telling you. You think, *If this were the right decision, I would feel peace. Since I feel terrible, I must have done something wrong.*

But that assumption is the trap.

In this chapter, we are going to learn a vital truth, one that might save you years of unnecessary striving: Guilt is not always a sign that you have sinned. Sometimes, it is just a sign that you have changed.

THE SHOCK COLLAR

To understand why we feel this way, we have to look at our internal wiring. It isn't just that you are "worrying" too much. It is a physical conditioning.

In Book 1, we talked about the alarm system that screams "Danger!" when you feel abandoned. But the Fawn response has a different kind of alarm. Think of it less like a siren and more like a **shock collar**.

For years, your nervous system learned that "Safety" equals "Keeping People Happy." The moment you set a boundary or disappoint someone, your system anticipates a shock, rejection, anger, or withdrawal. That sick feeling in your gut isn't alerting you to a fire; it's a conditioned reflex trying to zap you back into submission before you get hurt.

This isn't just "worry"; this is the physical weight of the Fawn response, your body's desperate attempt to reconnect by becoming small and compliant.

If you have spent your life as a people-pleaser, an over-functioner, or a peacekeeper, you have worn this collar for a long time.

Saying "no" = *Zap*. Disappointing someone = *Zap*. Resting when there is work to be done = *Zap*. Someone else's anger = *Zap*.

So, when you finally do the healthy thing, when you finally open the window to get some fresh air because you are suffocating under the weight of everyone else's needs, your system reacts. You feel that rush of heavy dread and the sinking sensation in your stomach.

This is not the Holy Spirit convicting you of sin. This is your nervous system reacting to a broken rule. You broke the invisible rule that says, "I must keep everyone happy to be safe."

The shock is real, but it is a false alarm. Just because you feel the zap doesn't mean you crossed a moral line. It just means you are doing something new.

THE "GOOD CHRISTIAN" CONDITIONING

Where did we get this wiring? It didn't happen overnight. For many of us, the shock collar was installed layer by layer, sermon by sermon, family gathering by family gathering.

We were praised when we were "easy." We were applauded when we were "selfless." We learned early on that the most valuable thing we could be was low maintenance.

I remember a conversation with a friend who told me, "I grew up believing that 'Joy' meant Jesus, Others, Yourself. That was the order. If I ever put myself before Others, I was breaking the order. I was being un-joyful."

It's a catchy acronym, but it's terrible theology if taken to the extreme. It teaches us that our needs are essentially obstacles to our holiness. It trains us to view our own limitations as failures.

So when we reach adulthood, we have a reflex. When someone asks for something, our internal "Good Christian" script activates.

They need help? I must help. They are sad? I must fix it. They are mad? I must apologize.

We become allergic to disappointing people. And because we equate disappointing people with disappointing God, the stakes feel impossibly high. We aren't just saying no to a potluck; we feel like we are saying no to our identity as a faithful believer.

This is why the guilt feels so physical. It's primal. It's the fear of being cast out of the tribe. But here is the good news: You can remove the collar.

Case Study: The Holiday Burnout

I want to introduce you to a friend of mine named Jessica. Jessica is the kind of person who makes holidays magical. She loves the lights, the music, and the way the church smells like pine needles and wax.

But every year, Jessica was miserable by December 25th. Why? Because she was the unspoken keeper of the traditions.

She made the three different kinds of cookies her grandmother used to make (even though she didn't even like anise). She hosted the big family dinner for twenty people because her house was the biggest. She bought thoughtful gifts for every niece, nephew, and second cousin. She attended every Advent service, volunteered for the pageant, and hand-wrote cards.

One year, disaster struck. Jessica got the flu in mid-November. It was a bad one, the kind that leaves you weak and shaky for weeks. By early December, she was still exhausted. She realized, with a sinking feeling, that she physically couldn't do "The Full Jessica Christmas."

She agonized over it for three days. She prayed about it. Finally, she typed out a text to her family group chat. Her fingers felt heavy as she hit send:

"Hey everyone, I'm still recovering, and I don't have the energy to host the big dinner this year. I'm happy to come if someone else hosts, or we can just do a potluck at Mom's. Love you all."

It was a reasonable, necessary boundary. It was honest.

But ten minutes later, her phone pinged. It was her aunt. "Oh no! It won't feel like Christmas without your house. Are you sure? Maybe we can just come over and help you clean?"

Then her mom called. Her voice was soft, but the guilt was heavy. "I understand, honey, but your father was really looking forward to it. You know how he gets about tradition. He's going to be so sad."

Jessica wasn't being scolded. No one was yelling. But the weight of their disappointment hit her like a truck. She felt awful. She felt selfish.

She sat on her couch, staring at the Christmas tree, and that familiar wet concrete feeling filled her chest. The internal monologue began:

I'm ruining Christmas. I should just suck it up. I can rest in January. It's only one day. Why am I being so weak? Mom is right; Dad will be crushed.

She was shutting down. She was literally thumbing out the text: "Never mind, I'll figure it out," when her husband gently took the phone out of her hand.

"Jessica," he said, looking her in the eye. "You aren't ruining Christmas. You are recovering from the flu. Feeling guilty doesn't mean you're wrong. It just means you care."

Jessica kept the boundary. And you know what? Christmas happened.

They ordered Chinese food at her mom's house. It was weird. It was different. Her aunt made a few passive-aggressive comments about the lack of homemade pie ("Store-bought is fine, I suppose..."). Her dad looked a little wistful.

But Jessica was asleep in her own bed by 9:00 PM. She didn't spend the day frantic and sweating in the kitchen. And for the first time in a decade, she didn't wake up on December 26th with a migraine.

The guilt she felt wasn't a signal that she had sinned against her family. It was just the discomfort of changing a pattern. Her family survived. The holiday survived. And Jessica survived.

CONVICTION VS. CONDEMNATION (KNOWING THE DIFFERENCE)

For those of us who want to honor God, this is where it gets tricky. We are terrified of ignoring our conscience. We worry, *What if this guilt IS God telling me I'm being selfish?*

We need to learn to distinguish between two very different voices: Holy Conviction and Fear-Based Guilt (Condemnation).

They feel similar at first; they both hurt, but they come from different sources and lead to very different places.

1. The Voice of Fear-Based Guilt (Condemnation)

- **It feels:** Heavy, chaotic, sludgy, and vague. It feels like a fog you can't see through. It produces a "shut down" or "freeze" response.
- **It sounds like:** "You are such a disappointment." "You're messing everything up." "You're a bad friend/mom/Christian." "Fix it NOW." "If you don't do this, they won't love you."
- **The focus:** It focuses on you and your shame. It attacks your identity.
- **The result:** It leads to hiding, numbness, or over-working to "earn" your way back into favor. It creates distance between you and God because you feel unworthy.

2. The Voice of Holy Conviction

- **It feels:** Sharp but clean. Clear. Specific. It feels like a light turning on in a dark room.
- **It sounds like:** "That tone of voice was unkind; go apologize." "You committed to this; you need to follow through." "You are ignoring your family to impress strangers."
- **The focus:** It focuses on restoration and truth. It attacks the behavior, not the person.
- **The result:** It leads to repentance, action, and peace. It draws you closer to God because you want to be aligned with Him.

Scripture tells us, "There is therefore now no condemnation for those who are in Christ Jesus" (Romans 8:1). If the voice in your head is condemning you, attacking your identity, making you feel worthless, or driving you into a slump of dread, that is not God.

God does not guilt-trip. He guides.

When Jessica felt guilty about Christmas, the voice wasn't saying, "Jessica, you made a vow to host dinner, and you are breaking it." (That would be conviction). The voice was saying, "You are disappointing everyone, and you are not enough." (That is condemnation).

The Theology of Loads vs. Burdens

There is another theological trap we fall into: The "Bear One Another's Burdens" trap.

We read Galatians 6:2: "Carry each other's burdens, and in this way you will fulfill the law of Christ." And we think, *Okay, that means I have to carry everything for everyone.*

But we stop reading too soon. Just a few verses later, in Galatians 6:5, it says: "For each one should carry their own own load."

Wait. Which is it? Carry each other's burdens, or carry your own load?

The Greek words used here tell the story.

The word for **Burden** (*baros*) refers to a crushing weight, something too heavy for one person to carry alone. A tragedy, a crisis, a sudden illness. These are the things we help each other with. We help a friend move a piano; we don't move it alone.

The word for **Load** (*phortion*) refers to a soldier's pack or a traveler's knapsack. It is the daily, manageable weight that each person is responsible for carrying themselves. Their emotions, their choices, their daily responsibilities.

The problem arises when we try to carry someone else's **Load** (their knapsack) and call it a **Burden**.

When you take responsibility for your mother's happiness, you are trying to carry her knapsack. When you constantly rescue a friend from the consequences of their own poor planning, you are carrying their knapsack.

That is not love; that is enabling. And it creates a dynamic where you are exhausted (carrying two packs), and they are weakened (carrying none).

Jesus calls us to help with burdens, not to steal loads. Setting a boundary is often just handing someone back their own knapsack and saying, "I believe you are strong enough to carry this."

THE "DENY YOURSELF" CONFUSION

We can't talk about Christian guilt without addressing the elephant in the room: Mark 8:34. *"Whoever wants to be my disciple must deny themselves and take up their cross and follow me."*

This verse has been used as a weapon against women's boundaries for centuries. We have been taught that "deny yourself" means "you should never have a preference, a need, or a limit."

But let's look at the context. Jesus was calling disciples to lay down their lives for the Gospel, to choose the Kingdom of God over the kingdom of the world. He was talking about surrendering our will to God's will.

He was not saying, "If your toxic relative wants to scream at you for an hour, you must sit there and take it because you don't matter." He was not saying, "You should destroy the body I gave you by working yourself into an early grave."

There is a massive difference between **Self-Denial** (choosing holiness over comfort) and **Self-Destruction** (erasing your personhood to keep people happy).

God created you with limits. He made you need sleep. He made you need food. He gave you emotions that signal when something is unsafe. Ignoring those signals isn't spiritual maturity; it's poor stewardship.

You cannot pour from an empty cup. And contrary to popular belief, God isn't asking you to pour until you break the cup. He wants you to be a vessel that lasts.

The "False Guilt" Checklist

Sometimes, we feel guilty about things that aren't actually moral failures. We feel guilty simply because we are human.

Let's look at a checklist of False Guilt. If you feel guilty about any of these, you can safely release it. These are not sins; they are limits.

You are NOT guilty for:

- Needing rest. (Jesus slept in storms.)
- Being sick. (Your body is not a machine.)
- Feeling overwhelmed. (It is a signal, not a sin.)
- Someone else's reaction to your boundary. (Their disappointment is their load/knapsack, not yours.)
- Not having money to lend. (You cannot give what you do not have.)

- Changing your mind. (You are allowed to reassess based on new information.)
- Taking time to think. (Wisdom requires pause.)
- Not being "nice" all the time. (Kindness and niceness are different; we'll talk about this in the next chapter.)

THE GUILT HANGOVER: MANAGING THE AFTERMATH

So, you've identified the False Guilt. You've remembered the Backpack Theory. But you still feel bad.

This is what I call the **Guilt Hangover**. It's that lingering, sinking feeling after you've set a hard boundary.

When this happens, don't try to "fix" the feeling. Don't run from it. And definitely don't pick up the phone to undo your boundary just to make the feeling stop.

Instead, talk to yourself. You need a script for your internal monologue.

- When the internal voice says: "You are so mean. Look how sad they are."
  - You answer: "I am not mean; I am clear. Their sadness is allowed, and my boundary is allowed. Both can exist."
- When the voice says: "You should have just done it. It would have been easier."
  - You answer: "Easier for them, but costly for me. I am choosing honest discomfort over resentful peace."
- When the voice says: "God is disappointed in you."
  - You answer: "God delights in truth. I am being truthful. I am stewarding the heart He gave me."

The Guilt Audit: A Tool for the Moment

So, what do you do when the guilt wave hits? You've said "no," and now you feel the weight pressing down on you.

Don't run from the feeling. Don't numb it with scrolling or food. Instead, pause and do a Guilt Audit. Ask these three questions:

1. Did I violate a core value or a promise?

- **If Yes:** (e.g., I promised I'd pick her up and I bailed because I just wanted to watch Netflix). Then apologize. That is healthy conviction. Make it right.
- **If No:** (e.g., I never promised to do this, they just expected me to). Then you are not guilty. You are just uncomfortable.

2. Is this guilt bringing me clarity or confusion? Does it tell me exactly what to fix? Or is it just a general cloud of "I'm bad"? Confusion usually comes from fear, not faith. Conviction is specific.

3. Am I feeling responsible for someone else's emotions? Am I feeling bad because I did something wrong, or because they are feeling sad? Remember: You are responsible *to* people, not *for* their feelings.

If you have done the Audit and found your guilt to be false, but your body is still trembling or feeling heavy, use this prayer to ground your nervous system.

Prayer for the Trembling Moment

"Father, my body is telling me I am in danger, but Your Word tells me I am safe. I feel the shaking of change, but I choose to stand on the Rock. I am not harming this person; I am stewarding the life You gave me. Quiet my alarm with Your peace. I am held. Amen."

The Boundary Builder: The Reframe Exercise

Let's practice this right now. I want you to look at a recent situation where you felt guilty.

The Situation: (e.g., I told my friend I couldn't go to her party.) **The Guilt Thought:** (e.g., "I'm being a bad friend. She's going to be lonely.")

Now, let's reframe it using **The Gatekeeper's Truth.**

The Gatekeeper's Truth: "I love my friend, but I have been out four nights this week, and I am exhausted. If I go, I will be resentful and disengaged. A good friend takes care of herself so she can be present. She is allowed to be disappointed, and I am allowed to rest."

Do you feel the difference? The guilt feels tight and frantic. The truth feels grounded and solid.

It takes practice. You are deactivating a lifetime of shock collars. But every time you withstand the guilt without caving, you are teaching your body a new truth: *I can have limits and still be loved. I can say no and still be good.*

You are safe. You are held. And you are allowed to close the window.

3

RESPONSIBILITY, NOT RESCUE

I f you are reading this book, I already know something about you. You have a high-definition radar for distress.

You can walk into a room and instantly sense if the tension is high. You know by the tone of a text message, just a single word, that your friend is spiraling. You can look at your spouse's shoulders and know they had a bad day at work before they even hang up their coat.

And because you notice it, you feel a magnetic pull to fix it.

This isn't because you are controlling (though that's often what boundaries books accuse you of). It is because you are caring. You have a heart that breaks for other people's breakage. When you see someone carrying a heavy load, your instinct is to run over and grab one of the handles.

But for many of us, that instinct has gone into overdrive. We haven't just grabbed a handle; we have picked up the whole couch.

We have confused caring *about* someone with *carrying* someone.

In this chapter, we are going to do some gentle but necessary surgery. We are going to separate two things that have likely been fused together in your heart for a long time: **Responsibility** and **Rescue**.

We often think they are the same thing. We think, *If I am a responsible friend/spouse/parent, I will rescue them from this mess.*

But the truth is, Rescue is often the enemy of Responsibility, both yours and theirs. Rescue is the exhausting work of trying to manage outcomes that don't belong to you. And nothing leads to burnout faster than trying to do God's job for Him.

The Anatomy of a "Fixer"

Let me introduce you to a woman I know named Maggie. Maggie is the person you want in your corner during a crisis. She is capable, smart, and has a heart the size of Texas.

Maggie has a younger brother, David, who has always struggled with jobs, with money, with relationships. For ten years, Maggie has been David's safety net.

When David couldn't make rent, Maggie "loaned" him the money (and we all know "loan" is a generous word here). When David got into a fight with his girlfriend, Maggie spent three hours on the phone talking him down. When David forgot to renew his car registration and got a ticket, Maggie was the one researching how to pay it online for him because he was "too stressed to deal with it."

Maggie told me over coffee one day, "I just want him to be okay. If I don't help him, everything falls apart. And I love him too much to watch him fall."

But if you looked closely at Maggie, she wasn't just a loving sister. She was depleted. She wasn't sleeping. She dreaded looking at her phone because every vibration felt like a lead weight dropping in her stomach. She was snapping at her husband and resentful of her own children's needs because she had poured all her emotional energy into David.

One afternoon, David called Maggie in a panic. He had lost another job. He was angry, blaming the boss, and demanding Maggie come over to help him update his resume immediately.

Maggie had a deadline for her own job that day. She had a migraine pulsing behind her eyes. But the old script kicked in: *He needs me. I have to go.*

She went. She wrote the resume. She calmed him down. She ordered him dinner.

And as she drove home that night, she didn't feel the "warm glow" of charity. She felt hollow. She felt a deep, numbing exhaustion. She realized that despite ten years of her "helping," David wasn't getting better. He was actually getting less competent. And she was disappearing.

Maggie was stuck in the Rescue Trap.

The Rescue Trap happens when we believe that our intervention is the only thing standing between our loved one and disaster. It feels like love, but it functions like anxiety.

PEOPLE-PLEASING IS PROTECTION

We need to talk about why we do this. Why did Maggie rush over there when she had a migraine? Why do you answer that phone call at 11:00 PM when you have to be up at 6:00 AM?

On the surface, it looks like generosity. But if we dig a little deeper, we often find that over-responsibility is a form of self-protection.

When you are an empathetic person, other people's stress feels like your stress. When they are anxious, a heavy blanket of dread settles over you. When they are sad, your own body goes numb.

So, we rush in to fix their problem, not just to help them, but to regulate our own nervous systems. We think, *If I can get them to calm down, then the heaviness in this room will lift, and I can finally breathe.*

This is a learned behavior. Many of us learned early on, perhaps in childhood, that we were safe only when the people around us were happy. We became experts at managing the emotional temperature of the room. We learned to "fawn", to merge with the needs of others to avoid conflict or disconnection.

We learned that being "good" meant being the shock absorber for everyone else's bumps in the road.

But here is the hard reality: You cannot manage someone else's emotions and your own integrity at the same time. Eventually, you have to choose.

RESPONSIBLE TO VS. RESPONSIBLE FOR

The way out of the Rescue Trap is to learn one vital grammatical distinction. It is the difference between the word **TO** and the word **FOR**.

In every relationship, you have a set of duties. But healthy boundaries require us to draw a line between what we are responsible to do, and what we are responsible for.

1. You are Responsible TO people. Being responsible *to* someone means you act with love, integrity, and kindness. It covers your behavior.

- You are responsible to be honest.
- You are responsible to be kind.
- You are responsible to keep your promises.
- You are responsible to show up when you say you will.
- You are responsible to listen when you have the capacity.

2. You are NOT Responsible FOR people. Being responsible *for* someone implies you are in control of their outcomes, their feelings, and their choices. (Unless you are the parent of a minor child, this list is much shorter than you think.)

- You are not responsible for their happiness.
- You are not responsible for their reaction to your boundary.

- You are not responsible for the consequences of their poor planning.
- You are not responsible for keeping them from feeling sad, angry, or disappointed.
- You are not responsible for their spiritual growth.

Let's go back to Maggie. Maggie was responsible *to* David. She was responsible to love him, to pray for him, and to be kind to him.

But she believed she was responsible *for* David. She thought she was responsible for his employment, his mood, and his financial survival.

THE SPIRITUAL DANGER: KNAPSACKS AND BOULDERS

As Christians, we often disguise our lack of boundaries as "bearing one another's burdens." We point to scripture to justify our exhaustion. But there is a fine line between being a servant and trying to be a savior.

To understand this, we need to look at Galatians 6. In the span of just a few verses, Paul seems to contradict himself.

In verse 2, he says, *"Bear one another's burdens, and so fulfill the law of Christ."* But in verse 5, he says, *"For each one shall bear his own load."*

Which is it? Do we help, or do we let them handle it?

The confusion clears up when we look at the Greek. The word for "burden" in verse 2 is *baros*. It refers to a heavy boulder, a crushing weight, like a sudden tragedy, a medical crisis, or profound grief. These are loads too heavy for one person to carry. We are absolutely called to help carry *boulders*.

But the word for "load" in verse 5 is *phortion*. This refers to a soldier's knapsack, his daily kit. It contains his own rations, his own supplies, his own responsibility. A soldier is expected to march carrying his own knapsack. If you try to carry another soldier's knapsack for him, you aren't helping him; you are weakening him.

Maggie was treating David's employment, which was his daily *knapsack*, as if it were a crushing *boulder*. She was carrying his kit for him.

When we constantly rescue people from their own knapsacks (the natural consequences of their choices), we are often getting in God's way. God has designed a world where cause and effect are excellent teachers. If I stay up all night, I am tired. If I spend all my money, I am broke. These consequences are the mechanisms God uses to wake us up.

When we rush in to cushion every fall, we are saying, "Here, let me put a pillow down so you don't feel the impact of that mistake."

We think this is self-denial. We think of Mark 8:34, where Jesus calls us to "deny ourselves." We interpret that as "deny your own needs to fix everyone else." But let me offer a reframe:

True self-denial is denying the urge to be the Hero.

It is denying the ego-boost of being the Savior. It is denying the control-freak part of us that thinks, *If I don't fix this, God will drop the ball.*

Ask yourself this hard question: Do I trust God enough to let this person struggle? Do I trust that He is working in their mess, even if I don't fix it?

THE SEE-SAW EFFECT: WHY THEY DON'T CHANGE

Have you ever noticed that in relationships where you over-function, the other person tends to under-function?

Picture a see-saw. If you work really hard to push your side up high, doing all the planning, all the emotional regulating, all the apologizing, all the fixing, the other person has to go down. They become passive. They become helpless.

Why should David learn to update his resume if he knows Maggie will do it better and faster? Why should your friend learn to self-soothe her anxiety if she knows you will talk her off the ledge for two hours?

By over-functioning, we unintentionally train people to depend on us. We create the very dynamic we resent. As long as you are carrying 150% of the emotional load, they only have to carry -50%.

The most loving thing Maggie could have done for David was to hand him back his own life.

What Support Actually Looks Like (vs. Rescue)

So, if we stop rescuing, does that mean we stop caring? Do we become cold and heartless?

Absolutely not. We shift from Rescue to Support.

- **Rescue says:** "You are in trouble; move over, I'll fix it."
- **Support says:** "I see you are in trouble; I believe you can figure this out, and I'm here to cheer you on."
- **Rescue says:** "I am anxious because you are anxious."
- **Support says:** "I can see you are anxious, but I am calm."
- **Rescue says:** "I will do it for you."
- **Support says:** "I will sit with you while you do it."

Imagine the difference if Maggie had used Support instead of Rescue.

- **Rescue:** Maggie writes the resume while David plays video games to de-stress.
- **Support:** Maggie says, "I love you, and I know losing your job is scary. I can't write your resume for you, but I can pray for you, and I'm free next Tuesday for coffee if you want to show me what you've written."

Do you feel the difference? Rescue is heavy; it feels like dragging someone uphill. Support is lighter; it feels like walking next to someone who is carrying their own pack.

THE BOUNDARY BUILDER

I want us to get very practical, because these habits are deeply ingrained. When we are in the heat of the moment, everything feels like "our job." We need a way to visually sort the laundry of life using the principle of the Knapsack and the Boulder.

Grab a piece of paper. We are going to sort your current stressors into three categories.

1. My Knapsack (My Responsibility) These are the daily loads that belong to you. You cannot give these away.

- My words and tone of voice.
- My boundaries (what I say yes or no to).
- My energy levels and need for rest.
- My own feelings and reactions.
- Keeping my side of the street clean.

2. Their Knapsack (Their Responsibility) These are the daily loads that belong to the other person. If you pick these up, you are stealing their growth.

- Their happiness or unhappiness.
- Their reaction to my boundary (anger, silence, guilt-tripping).
- Their financial choices.
- Their health management.
- Their relationship conflicts with others.
- The consequences of their actions.

3. The Boulder (God's Domain) These are the heavy weights of outcome, heart-change, and timing. These are too heavy for any human to manipulate.

- Whether or not they change.
- The timing of their breakthrough.
- Protecting them from every possible harm.
- Changing their heart.
- The ultimate plan for their life.

Look at your paper. If you are feeling that heavy dread or exhaustion, I guarantee it is because you have been trying to squeeze items from List 2 and List 3 into your own Knapsack.

You have been trying to carry their daily load (List 2) and God's outcome (List 3).

The work of this chapter is simple but profound: **Take everything out of your knapsack that doesn't belong there.**

Visualize yourself physically handing those things back. *"David, I am handing you back your career. This is your knapsack." "Mom, I am handing you back your loneliness. I cannot fill that void." "Lord, I am handing you the outcome of this situation. This is a boulder only You can move."*

When you do this, you will feel a weight lift off your chest. That weight was never yours to carry.

A New Definition of a Good Friend

We need to rewrite the script on what it means to be a "good" Christian friend, partner, or parent.

- **Old Script:** A good friend never says no, fixes every problem, and carries every burden.
- **New Script:** A good friend loves honestly, respects the other

person's autonomy, and trusts God enough to get out of the way.

When Maggie finally stopped fixing David's life, it was messy. He was angry. He accused her of not caring. He struggled for a long time.

But eventually, he learned how to pay a bill. He learned how to keep a job for more than three months. He stood up taller because he was finally carrying his own weight.

And Maggie? She got her life back. She started sleeping. She enjoyed her husband again. And when she did spend time with David, she wasn't looking at him as a project to be managed. She was looking at him as a brother to be loved.

You can care deeply. You can love wildly. You can serve generously. But you can only do those things for the long haul if you refuse to carry what is not yours.

The Boundary Builder: Action Step

Before we move to the next chapter, let's take a breath. Unlearning the "Savior" role is scary. It feels like taking the training wheels off a bike; you worry everyone is going to crash.

Take a pen and answer these two questions:

1. **Who is the person I feel most exhausted by right now?**
2. **What is one specific "Knapsack" item I am carrying for them that they are capable of carrying themselves?**
   (*Examples: Reminding them of appointments, giving them money, mediating their arguments, listening to the same vent session for the 100th time*).

Write it down. Name it as Rescue. And give yourself permission to put it down.

You are not abandoning them. You are simply retiring from the position of General Manager of the Universe. And the good news is that position was already filled.

4

LOVE, AVAILABILITY, AND THE MYTH OF LIMITLESS GIVING

We need to talk about the "Open" sign.

You know the one. It hangs in the window of your soul, glowing neon red, buzzing slightly, signaling to the world: *I am here. I am ready. I am open for business.*

For many of us, that sign has been on for a decade. We haven't flipped it to "Closed" since the early 2000s. We have convinced ourselves that the brightness of that sign is the measure of our love. We believe in a very specific, very dangerous equation:

- If I am loving, I will be available.
- If I am available, I will be needed.
- If I am needed, I am safe (and good, and faithful).

We treat our lives like a 24-hour convenience store. We think that to be a good friend, a good spouse, a good parent, or a good Christian, we must offer access to our time, energy, and emotions on demand, regardless of the hour or the cost.

But here is the problem with convenience stores: the lights are harsh, the doors never lock, and the person behind the counter is usually exhausted.

In this chapter, we are going to tackle the myth of Limitless Giving. We are going to separate the idea of Availability from the idea of Presence. And we are going to look at why keeping the "Open" sign on 24/7 isn't an act of heroic love, it's a recipe for bankruptcy.

THE GUY WHO DID EVERYTHING (MEET DAVID)

I want to introduce you to a friend of mine named David.

David is the guy you want on your team. He is a "salt of the earth" kind of man, steady, capable, and deeply committed to his faith. At church, David is the first one to arrive to set up chairs and the last one to leave to lock the doors. At work, he is the manager whose door is literally always open. His team knows they can Slack him at 9:00 PM, and he will reply within five minutes.

To the outside world, David looks like a pillar of strength. He looks like a servant leader.

But if you sat down with David for coffee (which was hard to schedule, because his calendar looked like a game of Tetris gone wrong), you would see something different in his eyes. You would see a man who is physically present but spiritually hollowed out.

One Sunday, David hit a wall. It wasn't a dramatic explosion; it was a quiet implosion.

He was standing in the lobby at church, listening to a couple tell him about their marital struggles. He was nodding. He was saying, "Mmhmm." He was doing all the things a good, supportive friend does. But inside, a heavy fog had settled over his mind.

> *I don't care. I literally do not care about your argument. I just want to go home and sit in a dark room.*

The thought washed over him with a cold dread. *What kind of monster am I?* he thought. *These are my friends. They are hurting. Why am I so numb?*

Later that afternoon, his wife asked him a simple question about their upcoming vacation. David didn't yell, but he slumped against the kitchen counter, his voice sounding flat and defeated. "I don't know, okay? Can I just have five minutes where nobody needs anything from me?"

The silence that followed was deafening.

David wasn't a monster. And he wasn't unloving. David was a man who had confused Capacity with Character. He believed that because he *wanted* to help everyone, he should be *able* to help everyone. He thought that saying "I'm unavailable" was synonymous with saying "I don't love you."

So, he kept giving. He gave from his reserves. Then he gave from his emergency tank. Then he gave from the fumes. And finally, when the tank was bone dry, he was shocked to find that the car wouldn't run.

David was suffering from the Myth of Limitless Giving.

The Difference Between Availability and Presence

We often use the words "available" and "present" interchangeably, but they are actually opposites in this context.

Availability is about access. It is logistical. It means your phone is on, your door is unlocked, and your body is in the room. It means you can be reached.

Presence is about engagement. It is relational. It means your heart is open, your mind is focused, and your spirit is settled enough to actually be with another person.

Here is the paradox: **The more indiscriminately available you are, the less truly present you can be.**

Think about David. Was he available to the couple in the church lobby? Yes. He was standing right there. He was accessible. But was he present? Absolutely not. His body was a shell; his mind was looking for an exit; his heart was barricaded behind a wall of exhaustion.

When we refuse to set limits on our availability, we eventually offer people the "Lite" version of ourselves. We offer them our distracted, resentful, half-listening selves. We give them the casserole, but we serve it with a side of bitterness. We pick up the phone, but we are scrolling through Instagram while they talk because we don't have the mental energy to focus.

We think we are being generous by saying yes, but we are actually short-changing them.

Real love requires presence. And presence requires energy. If you have spent all your energy being "available" to the demands of the universe, you have nothing left for the holy work of being present with the people who matter most.

THE THEOLOGY OF LIMITS (OR, WHY YOU AREN'T GOD)

Why do we do this? Why do we feel this compulsive need to be the "Open" sign?

For those of us with a faith background, the pressure is often spiritualized. We look at the nature of God, who is described as omnipresent (everywhere at once), omniscient (all-knowing), and omnipotent (all-powerful), and we subconsciously try to mimic Him.

We think *God never sleeps, so I shouldn't need to rest. God is always listening, so I should always answer my phone. God loves endlessly, so I should give until it hurts.*

But we are forgetting a critical distinction: **God is the Creator. You are the creature.**

God is infinite. You are finite. God is the ocean. You are a cup.

When a cup tries to hold the ocean, it doesn't become a bigger cup. It breaks.

God designed limits into the very fabric of creation. Have you ever noticed that God created night? He could have made a world of perpetual noon, where we could work and serve and "do" for 24 hours a day. But He didn't. He created a rhythm where, for roughly eight hours every single day, the lights go out. We are forced to lie down, close our eyes, and become completely unproductive.

Sleep is a daily act of humility. It is the moment we admit, "The world will have to spin without me for a while, because I am not God."

Even the land in the Old Testament was given a Sabbath. Every seven years, the fields had to lie fallow. They were not to be planted or harvested. Why? Because if you over-farm a field, if you demand that it produce a harvest year after year without rest, the soil loses its nutrients. It becomes dust. It stops producing anything at all.

David had become a field that had been farmed for ten years straight without a Sabbath. He wasn't "bad soil." He was just depleted soil.

The Myth of Limitless Giving tells us that our limits are a result of the Fall, that if we were just more spiritual, we wouldn't get tired. But Adam and Eve needed sleep before sin entered the world. Limits are not a sin. They are a design feature.

Acknowledging your limits isn't a lack of faith. It is an act of worship. It is acknowledging your station as a created being who relies on a Sustainer.

THE SLOW DRIFT: FROM GENEROSITY TO DEPLETION

Nobody wakes up one morning and decides, "I think I'll burn myself out today."

It happens slowly. It is a drift. It starts with a genuine heart of generosity. You love people. You want to help. You see a need, a volunteer gap at school, a friend moving house, a colleague overwhelmed with a project, and you step in. It feels good. It feels like love.

But without boundaries, generosity has a shelf life.

Over time, the "want to" quietly shifts into "have to." The joy of serving shifts into the pressure of maintaining. The "Open" sign starts to flicker.

I call this the Slide into Depletion. It happens in three stages:

- **Stage 1: The Wholehearted Yes.** This is sustainable giving. You see a need, you check your "knapsack" (remember Chapter 3?), you see you have the resources, and you give cheerfully. You feel energized by the helping. You go home tired but satisfied.
- **Stage 2: The Obligated Yes.** You are already at capacity, but someone asks. You feel a heaviness in your chest. You think, *I really shouldn't, but I don't want to let them down.* You say yes. You do the thing, but you feel a low-level hum of dread while doing it. You go home feeling drained and slightly irritable.
- **Stage 3: The Resentful Yes (Depletion).** You are empty. You have nothing left to give. But the "Availability Equation" kicks in: *If I say no, I am bad.* So you say yes. But now, you are numb. You are mentally keeping score ("I do everything for everyone and nobody does anything for me"). You are cynical. You are physically present but emotionally checked out. You go home and zone out with food, scrolling, or silence.

David was living in Stage 3. He was doing all the "right" things, but his heart had left the building years ago.

Sustainable Giving vs. Depleted Giving

How do you know where you are on that spectrum? It can be tricky, because on the outside, the actions look exactly the same. You are still baking the cookies; you are still leading the meeting; you are still answering the text.

The difference isn't in the action. It's in the source.

Generosity is life-giving when it flows from choice. It is draining when it flows from pressure.

Let's look at the difference side-by-side. I want you to read this list and be honest with yourself about which column represents your life right now.

Sustainable Giving (The "Overflow")

- **Motivation:** "I have resources to share, and I want to help."
- **Feeling while doing it:** Engaged, focused, warm.
- **Reaction to a "No":** If you had to say no, you would feel disappointment, but not crushing guilt.
- **Expectations:** You give freely without expecting a specific return.
- **Aftermath:** Tired, but a "good tired." You recover quickly.
- **Internal Monologue:** "I'm glad I could be there for them."

Depleted Giving (The "Deficit")

- **Motivation:** "If I don't do it, disaster will strike/they will hate me."
- **Feeling while doing it:** Heavy, numb, resentful, distracted.
- **Reaction to a "No":** If you consider saying no, you feel a sinking dread or heavy shame.
- **Expectations:** You secretly feel they "owe" you; you feel taken for granted.

- **Aftermath:** Exhausted, "guilt hangover," cynical, takes days to recover.
- **Internal Monologue:** "Why does everyone always want a piece of me?"

If you found yourself nodding at the "Depleted" column, take a deep breath. You are not a bad person. You are simply a convenience store that has run out of inventory.

And the only way to restock the shelves is to lock the door for a while.

CLOSING THE SHOP: A PRACTICAL GUIDE

So, what do we do? Do we become hermits? Do we tell everyone to go away?

No. We just learn to operate with store hours.

When David realized he was hurting his wife and his own soul, he didn't quit his job or leave his church. He started small. He decided that he needed to establish "Closed" hours.

He set a rule: No work emails or "fix-it" texts after 7:00 PM.

The first night he did it, his phone buzzed at 7:15 PM. It was a volunteer from church with a "crisis" regarding the Sunday bulletin. David saw the notification. His stomach dropped, that familiar heaviness pressing on his chest. The old script kicked in: *I should just answer. It will only take a minute. If I don't, they'll think I'm slacking.*

But he remembered the commitment he made to his own sanity. He put the phone in a drawer. He went back to eating dinner with his wife. He looked her in the eye. He listened to her story about her day. He was present.

He replied to the text the next morning at 8:30 AM. And guess what? The world hadn't ended. The bulletin got printed.

But something shifted in David. By "closing the shop" for the night, he reminded himself, and his community, that he was a human being, not an appliance.

You can do this too. You can decide that you are not available for heavy emotional processing via text message after 9:00 PM. You can decide that your lunch hour is for eating, not for catching up on favors. You can decide that you are not the emergency contact for every single person in your life.

The "Not Right Now" Script

The hardest part of turning off the "Open" sign is the moment someone pulls on the handle and finds the door locked. They might be surprised. They might knock.

Here is a script you can use when you are at capacity, but you still care:

> *"I care about you, and I want to hear about this, but I don't have the mental space to be fully present right now. Can we talk about this [tomorrow/on Tuesday] when I can actually focus?"*

Do you see what that does? It affirms the relationship (*I care about you*) while protecting the limit (*I don't have the space right now*). It moves you from Availability (answering half-heartedly now) to Presence (answering wholeheartedly later).

Love Thrives Within Limits

We have been terrified that limits will kill love. We think that if we draw a line, we are cutting off the flow of grace.

But the opposite is true. Limits are what make love sustainable.

Think of a river. A river needs banks. If you remove the banks, the boundaries ,the water doesn't flow stronger. It spreads out, becomes a swamp, and eventually dries up. The banks are what give the river its direction, its power, and its depth.

Your boundaries are the riverbanks of your love. They ensure that your love remains a flowing stream, deep and refreshing, rather than a stagnant, muddy swamp of resentment.

When you embrace your limits, you are not saying "I love you less." You are saying, "I want to love you for the long haul. I want to be a friend to you ten years from now, not just ten minutes from now. And to do that, I need to go to sleep."

David is still the guy who helps. He still sets up chairs sometimes. But he doesn't do it every week. And when he does, he smiles. A real smile. Because he is there by choice, not by compulsion. He turned off the neon sign, and in the darkness of rest, he found his light again.

THE BOUNDARY BUILDER: THE GIVING CHECK-IN

Before we move to Chapter 5, I want you to do a quick inventory. We often give on autopilot. We say "Yes" before our brain has even registered the request.

This week, before you agree to anything, a volunteer slot, a phone call, a coffee date, a favor, I want you to pause and ask these three questions.

1. **The Capacity Check:** "Do I have the time, energy, and resources to do this without going into debt relationally or physically?" (Be honest. If you are already running on fumes, the answer is no.)
2. **The Motive Check:** "Am I saying yes because I want to love this person, or because I want to avoid feeling guilty?" (If it's to avoid guilt, that is a "Resentful Yes" waiting to happen.)
3. **The Presence Check:** "If I say yes to this, can I actually be present? Or will I be physically there but emotionally absent?"

Write these on a sticky note. Put them on your mirror or your dashboard.

You are allowed to be a finite resource. You are allowed to have store hours. And you might just find that when you start respecting your own limits, the love you give becomes a lot more like the love God intended: cheerful, free, and real.

5

JESUS, DISCERNMENT, AND THE HOLY "NO"

We need to talk about the verses you have taped to your bathroom mirror.

You know the ones. They are written in beautiful calligraphy on a sticky note, or perhaps framed in a lovely font on your desk. They are the verses we cling to when the world feels heavy, and our energy feels light.

"I can do all things through Christ who strengthens me."

— (PHILIPPIANS 4:13)

"Do not grow weary in doing good."

— (GALATIANS 6:9)

These are powerful, life-giving promises. But for the woman who struggles with boundaries, they can easily become taskmasters. We read "I can do all things," and we interpret it as "I *should* do all things." We read "Do not grow weary," and we hear "You are not allowed to be tired."

We have sketched a cultural portrait of the "Good Christian Woman" that looks suspiciously like a superhero without a cape or boundaries. She never stops. She never sleeps. She is always available, always pouring out, always saying yes to the church bake sale, the late-night crisis call, the extra project at work, and the meal train.

And when she inevitably hits the wall of her own humanity, when she snaps at her kids, or cries in her car, or feels that hollow ache of burnout, she doesn't blame the schedule. She blames her faith. She thinks, *If I were just spiritual enough, I wouldn't be this tired. If I really trusted God, I would have the strength to do it all.*

In this chapter, we are going to dismantle that lie. We are going to look at the life of Jesus, not the Sunday School flannel-graph version, but the real, dusty, human Jesus of the Gospels, and discover a startling truth: **The Savior of the world said "No." A lot.**

And if He did, maybe it's time you learned how to, too.

THE FEAR OF MISSING OUT ON GOD (MEET HANNAH)

I want to introduce you to Hannah.

Hannah is the woman who is paralyzed by the thought that if she says "No," she is going to miss the boat. She isn't driven by ego; she is driven by a deep-seated compulsion to be used by God. Hannah views every request as a divine assignment.

If the children's ministry director asks for volunteers? *That's God calling.* If a neighbor mentions they are moving? *That's a divine appointment.* If her boss asks who can stay late? *That's an opportunity to be salt and light.*

Hannah's calendar looks like a game of Tetris played at the highest speed level. There are no gaps. Every white space has been filled with a coffee date, a service project, or a meeting. She lives with a heavy blanket of obligation that whispers, *What if I say no to this, and it was the thing God wanted me to do? What if I miss my purpose because I was too lazy to show up?*

Last year, Hannah was asked to lead a women's Bible study on Tuesday nights. Now, Hannah hates Tuesday nights. Tuesdays are her busiest days at work. By 5:00 PM, her brain is mush. She knew, deep in her bones, that she didn't have the capacity to lead a group of twelve women through a dense study of Romans.

She stood in the church lobby, clutching her purse. Instead of panic, she felt that familiar heaviness settle in her gut. Her shoulders slumped. A wave of numbness washed over her. She wanted to say, "I'm honored, but I can't right now."

But then the internal sermon started.

"Look at the harvest," the voice in her head said. *"The laborers are few. Who else will do it? If you say no, these women won't get led. Besides, 'I can do all things,' right? God doesn't call the equipped; He equips the called."*

So Hannah smiled a tight, plastic smile and said, "I'd love to."

Fast forward six weeks. Hannah wasn't "equipped." She was exhausted. She was prepping lessons at 1:00 AM, resentful and weeping over her open Bible. She was showing up to the group unprepared and irritable. She was snapping at her husband when she got home.

Hannah was doing a "good thing." Leading a Bible study is a holy work. But for Hannah, in that season, it was not a *good* work. It was an act of disobedience to her own limits.

She thought she was serving God by saying yes. But in reality, she was serving her own fear, the fear that if she didn't do it all, God's plan would fall apart.

THE THEOLOGY OF JESUS'S "NO"

We often think of Jesus as the ultimate "Yes Man." We see Him touching lepers, feeding thousands, and walking for miles to reach the lost. And He did all of those things. But if we read the Gospels closely, we see that His ministry was defined just as much by what He *didn't* do as by what He did.

Jesus governed His life by Discernment, not by Urgency.

There are two specific stories in the book of Mark that I return to whenever I feel that "Hannah" dread settling in my stomach. They are stories that show us exactly how Jesus handled the crushing pressure of human need.

1. The Capernaum Morning (Mark 1:35–38)

Picture the scene. Jesus has had a massive day in Capernaum. He has been teaching, casting out demons, and healing Simon's mother-in-law. By sunset, the news has spread. The entire town has gathered at the door.

Imagine the noise. The crying of sick children. The desperate pleading of parents. Jesus stays up late, healing many. Finally, the crowd disperses, and He collapses into sleep.

But the next morning, before the sun is even up, Jesus is gone.

He isn't in the kitchen making coffee. He isn't setting up a triage tent for the people who didn't get healed the night before. He has walked out to a "solitary place" to pray.

Meanwhile, the disciples are in a frenzy. They wake up, see the line of people forming down the block, people with crutches, people with fevers, people with deep needs, and they realize their Leader is missing.

When they finally find Jesus sitting quietly on a hillside, they are exasperated. You can hear the accusation in their tone:

"Everyone is looking for you!"

— (MARK 1:37)

Translation: *"Jesus, what are you doing here? There are people waiting! You are the Messiah, get back down there and fix them!"*

This is the moment. This is the moment where the "Good Christian" script says Jesus should jump up, apologize for being selfish, and run back to the crowd.

But He doesn't.

Jesus looks at Simon. He hears the report of the needy crowd. And He says the most shocking thing imaginable:

"Let us go somewhere else, to the nearby villages, so I can preach there also. That is why I have come."

— (MARK 1:38)

Did you catch that? **Jesus left people unhealed.**

There were still sick people in Capernaum. There were still blind eyes and lame legs. The need was not met. The inbox was not empty. And yet, Jesus walked away.

Why? Was He cruel? Was He lazy? No. He was **tethered**.

Jesus knew His assignment. He knew that if He stayed in Capernaum and became the local doctor, He would miss his primary mission, which was to preach the Kingdom to the other towns. He said "No" to the immediate, screaming needs of the crowd so He could say "Yes" to the ultimate direction of the Father.

He disappointed people to stay true to His purpose. If the Son of God had to leave needs unmet to stay on mission, who are we to think we can meet every need that comes across our path?

2. The Sleeping Savior (Mark 4:35–40)

If the Capernaum story doesn't convince you, let's look at the boat.

Jesus and the disciples are crossing the Sea of Galilee. Jesus is exhausted. He goes to the back of the boat, finds a cushion, and falls into a deep sleep.

Then, the storm hits. This isn't a drizzle; it's a furious squall. Waves are breaking over the boat. The disciples, professional fishermen , are convinced they are going to drown.

And Jesus? He is asleep.

The disciples rush to the back of the boat and shake Him awake. And listen to their question. It is the same question the world asks us when we try to set a boundary:

> *"Teacher, **don't you care** if we drown?"*
>
> — (MARK 4:38)

Don't you care?

This is the weaponized question. It equates activity with caring.

- If you cared about the church, you'd volunteer.
- If you cared about our friendship, you'd answer the phone.
- If you cared about the family, you'd host the dinner.

The disciples believed that because Jesus was sleeping during a crisis, He must not care about them. But Jesus's sleep wasn't a lack of care; it was a boundary. He was human. He was tired. His body required rest, and He took it, even in the middle of a storm.

Jesus modeled that **Self-Care is not Sin.** He modeled that you can be in the middle of a crisis and still need to close your eyes. He showed us that the world can be falling apart, and you are still allowed to trust God enough to go to sleep.

DISCERNMENT VS. AVOIDANCE

Now, I can hear the objection forming in your mind.

> *"Okay, but I'm not Jesus. I don't have a messianic mission to preach to the next village. If I say no to leading the Bible study, isn't that just me being lazy? Isn't that just avoidance?"*

This is a crucial distinction. We are not talking about saying "No" so we can sit on the couch and watch reality TV for six hours every night. We are talking about the difference between Discernment and Avoidance.

Avoidance is saying no because you are afraid. You are afraid of the work, afraid of the intimacy, or afraid of failure. Avoidance is running *away* from your calling.

Discernment is saying no because you are focused. Discernment is running *toward* your calling, which requires you to say no to the distractions along the way.

Here is the hard truth: The enemy of the Best is usually the Good.

Satan doesn't usually tempt the "Good Christian Woman" with obvious sins. He tempts you with good opportunities. He tempts you to over-volunteer, over-commit, and over-serve until you are so diluted and exhausted that you are ineffective at the few things God actually asked you to do.

Discernment is the ability to ask: *"God, is this mine to do?"* Not "Can I do it?" (Capacity). Not "Is it a good thing?" (Morality). But "Is it my assignment?" (Vocation).

The Savior Complex: Trying to Be the Holy Spirit

When we refuse to say "No," we are often operating out of a hidden Savior Complex. We look at a need, a friend's messy marriage, a gap in the church nursery, a family member's financial crisis, and we think, *If I don't step in, it won't get fixed.*

We act as if we are the glue holding the universe together.

But let's look at the theology of the Trinity. There is the Father, the Son, and the Holy Spirit. **You are not the Fourth Person of the Trinity.**

You are not the Holy Spirit. It is not your job to convict people, change people, or comfort people in a way only God can. When we try to be everywhere and fix everything, we are stepping into God's lane.

Remember the "Solitary Place"? When Jesus walked away from the crowd in Capernaum, He was trusting the Father with the people He left behind. He was trusting that the Father loved those sick people even more than He did.

When you say "No" to a request, you are creating space for God to work. You are creating space for someone else to step up. Your "No" is an act of trust. It declares, "God, You are big enough to handle this without my help."

The Love of the Delay (The Lazarus Boundary)

If you still struggle with the idea that a boundary can be loving, we have to talk about Lazarus.

In John 11, Jesus receives urgent news. His dear friend Lazarus is dying. His sisters, Mary and Martha, send a messenger saying, "Lord, the one you love is sick."

The expectation is clear: Jesus should drop everything and run. That is what love does, right? Love rushes in. Love fixes it.

But look at the text. It contains one of the most confusing sequences of sentences in the Bible:

> "*Now Jesus loved Martha and her sister and Lazarus.* **So** *when he heard that Lazarus was sick, he stayed where he was two more days.*"

— (JOHN 11:5–6)

Read that again. He loved them... **SO** He stayed.

Because He loved them, He delayed. Because He loved them, He didn't rush in to **anesthetize** their suffering. He allowed Lazarus to die. He allowed Mary and Martha to go through the excruciating grief of a funeral, the confusion of feeling abandoned, and the pain of loss.

Why? Because He knew that the result of the delay, the resurrection of Lazarus, would be greater than an immediate healing. He knew that the glory God would get from raising the dead was better than the relief they would get from a healed fever.

Jesus's delay was a boundary. He refused to let the urgency of others dictate his timeline. He refused to let their panic become his command.

When you say, "I can't do that right now," or "I need to wait before I commit," you are walking in the footsteps of the Lazarus story. You are trusting that your "No" (or your "Not Yet") might actually lead to a greater work of God than your immediate "Yes."

Practical Application: The Holy Pause

So, how do we actually do this? How do we stop the runaway train of "Yes"?

We start with **The Holy Pause.**

Most of us say "Yes" out of a reflex. It's a knee-jerk reaction to relieve the tension of the moment. Someone asks, we feel the weight of their expectation, we feel our gut drop, so we agree just to make the feeling stop.

We need to break that reflex. We need to insert a speed bump between the Request and the Response.

Here is a rule I want you to adopt for the next 30 days: **Give no immediate answers.**

To any request, whether it's for a volunteer role, a favor, or a social event, your answer is the same: *"Thank you for asking. I need to look at my calendar and pray about my capacity. I will let you know by [Time]."*

This simple script buys you freedom. It allows you to step away from the pressure of the person's face. And in that pause, I want you to ask two questions to distinguish between the Spirit and the Flesh.

1. The "Check" (Conviction/Wisdom): What does your spirit feel like when you think about doing this? Does it feel heavy, dark, or dread-filled? Do you feel a physical slumping in your posture? Often, the Holy Spirit leads us through peace. If there is no peace, that is a caution light. A "check" in your spirit is often God saying, "Don't go there."

2. The "Fear" (Anxiety/People-Pleasing): What are you afraid will happen if you say no? *"They will be mad." "They won't like me." "I won't look like a good Christian."* If your motivation for saying "Yes" is fear, it is not from God.

The Detox Phase: When Being "Useless" Hurts

I want to be honest with you about what happens after you start using the "Holy Pause."

When you first stop the frantic cycle of "Yes," you won't feel peaceful. You will feel useless.

For years, your identity has probably been built on being the Reliability Rock. You get a dopamine hit every time you save the day. You feel significant when you are the one everyone calls. Being "The Helper" is a powerful drug.

When Hannah finally stepped down from the Bible study and stopped answering work emails after 6:00 PM, she didn't feel relief immediately. She felt an itch. She checked her phone constantly, even though it wasn't buzzing. She felt a phantom guilt, like she was forgetting to pick up a child from school, even though everyone was safe.

She told me, "I feel like I'm disappearing. If I'm not fixing things, do I even matter?"

This is the **Detox Phase.** It is the withdrawal symptom of a savior complex.

When you stop over-functioning, you are forced to confront the quiet. You are forced to confront the question: *Am I worthy of love simply because I exist, or only because I produce?*

If you feel the itch to jump back in and rescue someone, or if you feel the ache of "uselessness," don't run from it. Sit in it. That ache is your soul healing. It is your heart learning a new rhythm, one where you are loved not for your utility, but for your identity as a daughter of the King.

Let the phone ring. Let the email wait. You are not the Savior. And that is the best news of all.

The Gatekeeper's Truth

"No" is a complete sentence. You do not need to offer a 10-minute explanation, an apology, and three alternative solutions. You do not have to justify your limit to make it valid. Jesus didn't offer a seminar on burnout to the disciples when He went to sleep in the boat. He just slept. Your limits are not a sin to be confessed. They are a reality to be respected.

THE BOUNDARY BUILDER: THE "CALENDAR AUDIT"

Before you move to the next chapter, let's do a quick audit.

1. Take out your calendar for the next two weeks.
2. Circle every item that is an "optional obligation" (not your job, not your immediate family care).
3. Look at each circled item and ask: *If this got cancelled today, would I feel relieved or disappointed?*
   - If you would feel disappointed, keep it. That is a joy.
   - If you would feel relieved, that is a burden.
4. Choose **ONE** item from the "Relieved" list to cancel or step back from this week. Use the script: *"I've realized I don't have the capacity to give this the attention it deserves, so I need to step back."*

Do it. The world will keep spinning. God is still on the throne. And you might just get your soul back.

6

THE IDOL OF NICENESS VS.
THE POWER OF KINDNESS

"Faithful are the wounds of a friend; profuse are the kisses of an enemy."

— PROVERBS 27:6

M eet Becca.

If you met Becca in the lobby of your church or in the break-room at work, you would like her immediately. Everyone does. Becca is widely considered "the sweetest person I know."

She is the woman who always smiles, even when she is tired. She is the first to volunteer for the meal train, even when her own week is drowning in chaos. Her emails are peppered with exclamation points and emojis, usually three or four at a time, just to make sure you know she isn't upset, even when she is writing to correct a billing error or ask for a refund. She apologizes when she hasn't done anything wrong. She apologizes when you bump into her.

Becca has spent thirty-eight years perfecting the art of being "low maintenance." She has been conditioned to believe that her primary contribution to the Kingdom of God is to be pleasant.

But if you could see the interior of Becca's soul, you wouldn't see peace. You would see a pressure cooker.

Last month, Becca's friend **Hannah** called her, frantic. Hannah is currently dating a man whom Becca knows, deep in her bones, is bad news. He is dismissive, arrogant, and belittling. Hannah called to vent about their latest fight, looking for reassurance.

Becca sat on her kitchen floor, listening to Hannah justify his behavior for forty-five minutes. Becca felt a familiar heaviness settle over her chest. She knew the truth: *Hannah, this man is not safe for you. You need to get out.*

But Becca didn't say that.

Instead, Becca said, "Oh, wow. That sounds so hard. I'm so sorry you're going through that. Maybe he's just stressed with work?"

Becca hung up the phone feeling dirty. She felt a numbness spreading through her limbs. Later that night, she snapped at her husband for leaving his shoes in the hallway, an explosion of anger that seemed to come out of nowhere but was actually the displaced rage of a woman who had just lied to her best friend.

Becca believes she is being "nice." She believes she is keeping the peace. She believes that by swallowing her truth, she is loving Hannah well.

But Becca isn't being loving. Becca is being cowardly.

This is the hard reality we have to face in this chapter, and it might be the most uncomfortable pivot of the entire book. We have to talk about the difference between being Nice and being Kind.

For generations, Christian women have been handed a counterfeit version of the Fruit of the Spirit. We have been taught that "kindness" looks like compliance. We have been taught that to be Christlike is to be agreeable, soft-spoken, and endlessly accommodating. We have turned "Niceness" into an idol and bowed down to it, burdened by the heavy dread that if we stop smiling, we will lose our witness.

But if we look at the life of Jesus, and if we look at the true definition of love, we find something startling:

Niceness is not a Fruit of the Spirit.

Niceness is a social survival strategy. Kindness is a holy weapon. And until we learn the difference, our boundaries will always crumble under the weight of our fear.

THE ANATOMY OF NICENESS

Let's deconstruct what was actually happening with Becca on that phone call. Why did she lie? Why did she offer a soft, "nice" excuse for a man she knows is toxic?

She did it because she was in a state of self-preservation.

Becca was afraid that if she told the truth, *Hannah, I love you, but I can't listen to you complain about him anymore, if you aren't willing to leave him,* Hannah might get angry. Hannah might cry. Hannah might accuse Becca of being unsupportive or judgmental. The conversation would become "awkward," and Becca's body interprets "awkward" as "dangerous."

Niceness is almost always motivated by self-protection.

When we are operating out of Niceness, our internal monologue is focused on us:

- *How do I look right now?*
- *Do they like me?*
- *Am I making them uncomfortable?*
- *Will they think I'm mean?*
- *How can I escape this moment without conflict?*

Niceness is focused on managing the other person's reaction so that we can feel safe. It is superficial. It is focused on the immediate emotional climate. It prioritizes "smoothness" over everything else.

The problem with Niceness is that it is often dishonest. Becca wasn't listening to Hannah; she was enduring Hannah. She wasn't offering wisdom; she was offering a pacifier. By prioritizing the "nice" exterior, she sacrificed the truthful interior.

Niceness is the beautiful wrapping paper on an empty box. It looks good, it feels pleasant, but there is no substance inside. It is a form of emotional hiding. We hide our true thoughts, our true needs, and our true convictions behind a wall of agreeable smiles because we are paralyzed by the thought of rejection.

We have confused "keeping the peace" with "making peace."

Niceness keeps the peace by suppressing the truth. It pushes the dirt under the rug and pretends the room is clean. But as anyone who has ever cleaned a house knows, dirt under the rug doesn't disappear. It accumulates. Eventually, you trip over the mound.

THE THEOLOGY OF KINDNESS

Now, let's look at Kindness.

In Galatians 5:22-23, Paul lists the Fruit of the Spirit: "love, joy, peace, patience, kindness, goodness, faithfulness, gentleness, self-control."

The Greek word used for kindness here is *chrestotes*. It implies moral goodness, integrity, and a disposition that seeks the welfare of the other.

Notice the shift in focus.

- **Niceness is about ME** (my image, my comfort, my safety).
- **Kindness is about YOU** (your good, your growth, your healing).

True Kindness is fiercely other-centered. Because it is focused on the other person's ultimate good, Kindness is willing to risk the relationship to save the person. Kindness is willing to say the hard thing, to set the boundary, or to disrupt the false peace, because it knows that truth is the only thing that sets people free.

Let's look at Jesus. Was Jesus "nice"? If we are honest with the text of Scripture, the answer is frequently no.

Jesus was often incredibly inconvenient. He was disruptive. He was blunt.

In Matthew 16, when Peter tries to convince Jesus not to go to the cross, a very "nice," protective gesture, Jesus turns to him and says, "Get behind me, Satan! You are a stumbling block to me." That is not nice. That is a sharp, jagged rebuke. But it was Kind. He was cutting out the cancer of Peter's worldly thinking to save Peter's soul.

In Mark 11, Jesus enters the temple courts. He sees the money changers exploiting the poor and turning the house of prayer into a market. He doesn't write a polite email with three exclamation points asking them to please consider relocating. He braids a whip. He flips heavy tables. He drives them out. He yells.

Was Jesus sinning in the temple? Was He failing to show the Fruit of the Spirit? No. He was embodying fierce, protective Kindness.

He was disrupting a toxic status quo to establish true holiness. He wasn't worried about the money changers thinking He was "mean." He was worried about the vulnerable people being exploited. He was worried about the purity of God's house.

When we set a boundary, we are often flipping a table in our own lives.

When you tell your mother, "I can't speak to you when you yell at me; I'm hanging up now," you are flipping the table of abuse. When you tell a friend, "No, I can't loan you money again," you are flipping the table of irresponsibility.

It doesn't feel "nice." The other person will likely be offended, just as the money changers were surely offended. They might call you difficult. They might say you've changed.

But you are not called to be nice. You are called to be kind.

THE SURGEON VS. THE ENABLER

To understand this deeply, I want you to imagine two doctors.

Doctor A is the "Nice Doctor." You go to see him because you have a persistent pain in your side. He runs a scan and sees a tumor. He knows it is dangerous. But he looks at you, you seem so anxious, so fragile. He thinks, *If I tell her she needs surgery, she's going to be scared. It's going to hurt her. I don't want to be the bearer of bad news.*

So, Doctor A smiles warmly, hands you a lollipop, and says, "You're doing great! Just go home and get some rest. Don't worry about a thing."

You leave his office feeling relieved. You tell your friends, "He is such a nice doctor! He made me feel so much better."

Doctor B is the "Kind Surgeon." You go to her with the same pain. She runs the scan, sees the tumor, and sits you down. She looks you in the eye. Her face is serious.

She says, "I have hard news. You have a tumor. We need to operate immediately. I am going to have to cut you open. You will be in pain during recovery, and you will have a scar. But this is the only way to save your life."

You leave her office shaking. You are scared. You might even be angry that this is happening. You don't leave feeling "good."

But tell me: Which doctor actually loved you?

Doctor A, the "Nice Doctor," is actually cruel. His "niceness" was malpractice. By prioritizing your immediate emotional comfort over your ultimate reality, he sentenced you to death. He protected himself from the discomfort of your pain, but he failed to help you.

Doctor B, the "Kind Surgeon," inflicted pain. The scalpel hurts. The recovery hurts. But the wound she inflicted was a faithful wound. It was a wound designed to heal.

This is the distinction we miss in our relationships. When we refuse to set boundaries, when we engage in "codependent niceness", we are acting like Doctor A. We are handing out lollipops to people who are spiritually or emotionally sick.

- When you clean up your teenager's mess every time so they don't face consequences, you are the lollipop doctor. You are "nice," but you are robbing them of the capability to become a functioning adult.
- When you listen to your mother-in-law gossip about the rest of the family and nod along because you don't want to upset her, you are the lollipop doctor. You are enabling a sin pattern that is poisoning her soul and your family culture.
- When Becca told Hannah, "it's okay," she was the lollipop doctor. She smoothed over the symptom while the disease of the toxic relationship continued to rot.

Kindness is the Surgeon. Setting a boundary is the surgical cut.

- "I love you too much to watch you destroy yourself with this man. I cannot support this relationship anymore." (The Scalpel).
- "I will not allow you to speak to me that way. If it continues, I will leave." (The Scalpel).

It stings. It causes a rupture. The other person may react with pain ("I can't believe you're doing this to me!"). But this is the only way to move toward *Shalom*.

In Hebrew, *Shalom* means peace, but it doesn't mean "the absence of noise." It means wholeness. Completeness. Nothing missing, nothing broken. You cannot have *Shalom* without Truth.

"Toxic Peace" (appeasement) covers the wound. "Godly Peace" (Shalom) cleans the wound so it can close properly.

THE "MEAN GIRL" FEAR

I can feel the heaviness settling in your chest as you read this. I know the objection rising in your throat because I have whispered it to myself a thousand times:

"But if I act like the Surgeon... won't they think I'm a b-word?"

(Christian women usually don't say the word, even in our heads, but we feel the weight of it. We fear being labeled a Witch. A Shrew. A "Difficult Woman.")

We are burdened by the dread that if we drop the "Nice Girl" mask, we will reveal a monster. We worry that directness equals cruelty.

We have this backward.

I want to give you a mantra that changed my life, coined by researcher Brené Brown: **"Clear is Kind. Unclear is Unkind."**

Think about the times you have been hurt the most in relationships. Was it when someone looked you in the eye and clearly stated a limit? Or was it when someone smiled to your face but complained about you behind your back?

Was it when someone said, "I can't come to your party," or was it when they said, "I'll try!" and then ghosted you, leaving you wondering if you did something wrong?

Ambiguity is cruel. Hinting is cruel. Passive-aggression is cruel. Sighing loudly, hoping someone notices you are mad, is cruel. Expectations that are never spoken but always disappointed are cruel.

These behaviors create anxiety in the people around us. When we are "nice" but lacking boundaries, we force the people we love to walk on eggshells. They never know where they actually stand with us. They don't know if our "Yes" is a real "Yes" or a "Yes-with-resentment."

When Becca finally explodes at her friend (and she will), Hannah is going to be blindsided. She will say, "I thought you liked listening to me! You never said anything!" And Hannah will be right. Becca's "niceness" was actually a setup. She let Hannah believe everything was fine until it was too late.

Clarity, on the other hand, is a gift.

When you are clear, "I can't do dinner Tuesday, I need to rest", you give the other person the gift of knowing the truth. You release them from the job of mind-reading. You build trust.

People may not like the boundary in the moment, but they can trust the person who set it. They know that what you say is what you mean. Your "Yes" becomes solid ground because your "No" is a defined border.

You are not being a "Mean Girl" when you are direct. You are being a mature woman of God who respects herself and her neighbor enough to tell the truth.

PRACTICAL APPLICATION: THE "KIND HONESTY" SCRIPTS

So, how do we do this? How do we move from the Lollipop Doctor to the Kind Surgeon without becoming harsh?

The goal is Kind Honesty. This is the sweet spot where truth and love meet.

The formula generally looks like this: **Affirmation of the Person + Clarity of the Limit + Release of Outcome.**

You do not need to over-explain. You do not need to write three paragraphs of apology. You do not need to lie.

Here are some scripts to help you practice smashing the Idol of Niceness in your everyday life.

Scenario 1: The "I Don't Care" Trap

- **The Situation:** Your husband or friend asks where you want to eat or what you want to do. You have a preference, but you want to be "easy."
- **The Nice (Dishonest) Response:** "Oh, whatever you want is fine! I don't care." (Internal thought: *I really don't want tacos again, but I won't say that.*)
- **The Kind Honest Response:** "I have a strong preference for Italian tonight, but I'm flexible if you're craving something else."
- **Why this works:** It gives them data. It owns your desire. It allows for negotiation without erasure.

Scenario 2: The Capacity Check

- **The Situation:** A friend asks you to volunteer for a committee, or a family member asks for a favor you simply don't have the energy for.
- **The Nice (Dishonest) Response:** "Sure! I can probably squeeze that in!" (Followed by weeks of dread and resentment).
- **The Kind Honest Response:** "Thank you so much for thinking of me. I love what you're doing, but I don't have the capacity to give this the attention it deserves right now, so I need to decline."
- **Why this works:** You aren't rejecting them; you are acknowledging your limit. It honors the work by saying, "I can't do a good job at this, so I won't do it."

Scenario 3: The Drain

- **The Situation:** A friend is using you as an unpaid therapist. The conversation is one-sided and draining.
- **The Nice (Dishonest) Response:** Listening for two hours while interjecting "Uh-huh" and "Wow," then feeling depleted for the rest of the day.
- **The Kind Honest Response:** "I love you, and I want to support you, but I'm feeling really drained today and don't have the emotional space to process this right now. Can we talk about something lighter, or catch up on this next week?"
- **Why this works:** It protects the connection. If you don't say this, you will eventually stop answering her calls. Saying this keeps the friendship alive.

Scenario 4: The Pushback

- **The Situation:** You said no, and they are pushing. "Oh, come on, just this once! You're being selfish."
- **The Nice (Dishonest) Response:** Caving in. "Okay, fine, I guess I can."
- **The Kind Honest Response:** "I hear that you're disappointed, and I understand. But my answer is still no."
- **Why this works:** You validate their feeling ("I hear you") without taking responsibility for fixing it. You hold the line.

CLOSING: SMASHING THE IDOL

As we close this chapter, I want you to take a moment to look at the Idol of Niceness in your life.

It is a shiny, golden idol. It has promised you safety. It has promised you that if you just smile enough, apologize enough, and accommodate enough, you will be loved. It has promised that you can control how everyone feels about you.

But it is a lie.

The Idol of Niceness demands that you burn your own mental health, your own integrity, and your own authentic self on its altar. It leaves you hollow, resentful, and unknown.

God wants more for you. He does not want a "nice" daughter who secretly resents His people. He wants a Kind daughter who loves from a place of wholeness.

He wants you to be the Surgeon, not the Enabler. He wants you to be a Peacemaker, not a Peacekeeper.

It takes courage to stop being nice. The first time you send an email without an exclamation point, your stomach might drop. The first time you tell a friend, "I can't," you will feel a wave of guilt.

That guilt is not the voice of the Holy Spirit. That guilt is simply the withdrawal symptom of your addiction to approval.

Let it pass. Stand your ground.

You are learning a new language. You are learning the language of Jesus, who loved people enough to tell them the truth.

THE BOUNDARY BUILDER: THE NICENESS AUDIT

Before you turn the page, we need to do some inventory. We are going to identify where the Idol of Niceness is currently operating in your life.

Grab your journal or a piece of paper. I want you to answer these three questions with brutal honesty. No one else needs to see this.

1. **Where am I saying "Yes" when my heart is screaming "No"?**
   (Is it a specific relationship? A volunteer role? A family expectation?)
2. **Who am I currently "managing" or "enabling"?** (Who are

you offering lollipops to when they need surgery? Who are you afraid to be honest with because you fear their reaction?)

3. **Rewrite one script.** Pick one situation from above. Write down what you normally say (The Nice/Dishonest script). Now, look at the Kind Honesty examples and write down what you wish you could say. Just writing it down is the first step toward saying it.

Prayer for the Recovering Nice Girl: *Lord, forgive me for making an idol out of being liked. Forgive me for confusing my fear of man with the Fruit of the Spirit. Teach me the difference between being nice and being kind. Give me the courage to be a surgeon, to love others with truth, and to trust You with their reactions. Replace my cowardice with Your holy confidence. Amen.*

7

WHAT BOUNDARIES ACTUALLY ARE (THE GATE VS. THE WALL)

I f I asked you to close your eyes and picture a "boundary," what image comes to mind?

For most of the people I talk to, the image is stark. They picture a brick wall. A locked door. A "Keep Out" sign. Maybe even a moat with alligators circling the perimeter.

When we view boundaries through this lens, it makes sense why we avoid them. If you value connection, why would you build a wall? If you love people, why would you lock them out? If your faith is built on the concept of hospitality and welcoming the stranger, a "Keep Out" sign feels like a betrayal of your deepest values.

So, we swing to the other extreme. We tear down the fences. We leave the doors wide open. We let anyone walk through the living room of our lives with muddy boots, anytime they want, because we carry a deep **dread** that the only alternative is to sit alone in a fortress.

But this binary thinking, Wall or Nothing, is a trap.

In this chapter, we are going to replace that image. We are going to tear down the Brick Wall and replace it with something much more biblical, functional, and loving: **A Gate.**

- A wall says, "I don't want you here."
- A gate says, "I control access to here."

A wall is static; it separates forever. A gate is dynamic; it opens and closes based on wisdom, safety, and capacity.

When you have a gate, you are not cutting people off. You are simply installing a latch that allows you to decide who comes in, when they come in, and how long they stay.

This shift changes everything. It moves us from a posture of defense (keeping people away) to a posture of stewardship (taking care of what God has entrusted to us).

THE THEOLOGY OF THE YARD (OR, WHY GOD LOVES ORDER)

To understand boundaries, we have to look at the very beginning of the story.

If you turn to the first page of your Bible, Genesis 1, you see a picture of the world before God started His creative work. The text says the earth was "formless and empty," and "darkness was over the surface of the deep."

In Hebrew, the phrase is *tohu wa-bohu*. It means chaos. Confusion. A void where nothing can thrive because nothing is defined.

So, what is the very first thing God does to create a world where life can flourish? He draws lines. He makes distinctions. He sets boundaries.

- He separates the light from the darkness.
- He separates the water from the dry land.
- He separates the day from the night.

God did not look at the chaos and say, "Well, I don't want to be mean to the water, so I'll just let it go wherever it wants." No. He said to the sea, "This far you may come and no farther; here is where your proud waves halt" (Job 38:11).

By creating boundaries, God created order. And within that order, life exploded. Plants could grow. Animals could run. Humans could breathe.

Life cannot thrive in a void. Life requires structure.

Your life is a garden entrusted to you by God. It has soil (your heart), resources (your energy and time), and fruit (the love and service you offer the world).

If that garden has no fences, if your neighbor can drive their truck through your flowerbeds, if stray dogs can dig up your vegetables, if anyone can dump their trash on your lawn, you do not have a garden. You have a vacant lot. You have *tohu wa-bohu*.

Boundaries are simply the property lines that define where your garden begins and ends. They define what you are responsible **for** and what you are responsible **to**.

THE PROPERTY LINE PRINCIPLE

Let's make this concrete. Imagine you own a house with a yard.

You are responsible for what happens inside your property line. You mow the grass. You water the flowers. If a window breaks, you fix it. You are the steward of that space.

Your neighbor also has a yard.

Now, imagine your neighbor hates mowing his grass. He ignores it for weeks. It gets three feet high. It looks terrible.

If you are a person with "porous" boundaries (no fence), you might look at his yard and feel a heavy weight of obligation. You feel unsettled by the mess. You rush over to mow it for him, thinking, *I'm being helpful!*

But if you do that every week, two things happen:

1. **You get exhausted.** You are now maintaining two yards with the energy meant for one. Your own yard starts to suffer because you are too tired to tend it.
2. **He gets lazy.** Why should he mow his grass? You're doing it. You have robbed him of the responsibility of stewardship.

Boundaries help us clarify ownership.

- Let's look at **My Yard**, which is my responsibility. This includes things like: My feelings. My attitudes. My behaviors. My choices. My body. My time. My relationship with God.
- Now let's look at **Your Yard**, which is *your* responsibility. This includes: Your feelings. Your attitudes. Your behaviors. Your choices. Your body. Your time. Your relationship with God.

When we confuse these yards, we get into trouble.

We think, *I am responsible for his anger.* (No, his anger is in his yard.) We think, *I am responsible for her loneliness.* (No, her loneliness is in her yard.) We think, *I am responsible for their financial crisis.* (No, their spending habits are in their yard.)

This doesn't mean we don't care. If your neighbor breaks his leg, you go over and mow his grass. That is love. That is bearing a burden (Galatians 6:2).

But if your neighbor just prefers watching football to mowing grass, and you do it for him because you feel a sense of dread that he won't like you if you don't? That is not love. That is a lack of boundaries. That is trying to steward property you do not own.

The Three Boundary Styles: A Case Study

To see how this plays out in real life, let's look at three different ways people handle their "yards."

Meet Mark.

Mark is a good guy. He is a faithful husband, a dedicated employee, and a deacon at his church. He loves God and wants to serve people. But Mark is tired. Deeply, soul-achingly tired.

Mark has a coworker, Steve, who is constantly disorganized. Steve misses deadlines, forgets to prep for meetings, and is always in a "crisis" at 4:30 PM on a Friday.

Let's look at how Mark handles Steve in three different scenarios.

Style 1: The Porous Boundary (The Doormat)

In this version, Mark has no fence. His yard is open territory.

When Steve rushes in at 4:30 PM on Friday, saying, "Mark, I totally forgot the quarterly report is due! You have to help me, or I'm dead," Mark feels a **familiar heaviness settle in his chest**.

He promised his wife, **Rachel**, he'd be home early for dinner. He is exhausted. But Mark thinks, *If I say no, Steve will be mad. I can't handle that tension. That wouldn't be very Christian of me.*

He feels his shoulders slump. He goes numb to his own needs.

So Mark says, "Okay, sure. I can stay."

Mark does Steve's work. He misses dinner with **Rachel**. He goes home resentful, snaps at his kids, and lies awake at night fuming. Steve learns nothing and repeats the crisis next week.

The Result: Mark's yard is trampled. He is full of bitterness. The relationship with Steve is preserved on the surface, but underneath, Mark is starting to hate him.

Style 2: The Rigid Boundary (The Fortress)

Now, let's imagine Mark swings to the other extreme. He reads a book on boundaries (maybe this one!) and gets angry. He decides he is done being used. He builds a ten-foot concrete wall topped with razor wire.

When Steve comes in at 4:30 PM, Mark doesn't even look up from his desk. He says, "Not my problem, Steve. You should have planned better. I'm leaving at 5:00. Good luck."

He packs his bag and walks out while Steve stands there, panic-stricken.

Mark goes home. He made it to dinner. But he feels cold. He feels hard. When Steve tries to talk to him on Monday, Mark is short and defensive. He has protected his time, but he has severed the connection. He is safe, but he is isolated.

The Result: Mark's yard is pristine, but it is a lonely place. He has protected himself, but he has lost his influence and his warmth.

Style 3: The Healthy Boundary (The Gate)

This is the goal. This is the sweet spot.

Mark installs a picket fence with a sturdy gate. He clearly defines his property line, but he keeps the latch accessible.

When Steve comes in at 4:30 PM, Mark pauses. He checks his own yard (his capacity, his prior commitment to **Rachel**). He realizes he cannot fix this for Steve.

He looks Steve in the eye and speaks with kindness, but firmness.

"Steve, I can see you're really stressed. That's a tough spot to be in. However, I have a commitment to my family tonight, so I cannot stay and help you write the report."

(He pauses. He does not apologize for having a life. He waits through the awkward silence, even though it makes him want to squirm.

"I am available for fifteen minutes right now to help you outline a plan to get it done, but I have to walk out the door at 5:00."

The Result: Mark has protected his yard (he goes home to his family). He has returned Steve's load to Steve's yard (Steve has to do the work). But he has kept the gate open for connection (he offered fifteen minutes of support).

Steve might be unhappy. He might fail. But Mark has acted with integrity. He has offered love without offering rescue.

What Are We Actually Fencing In?

When we talk about installing these gates, it helps to know exactly what we are protecting. You aren't just protecting "your time." You are protecting the entirety of your personhood.

Here are the four main categories where your property lines need to be clear.

1. Physical Boundaries (Your Body and Space) This is your most basic property line. It defines who can touch you, how close they can get, and how your physical body is treated.

- **Personal Space:** Stepping back when someone stands too close.
- **Touch:** Saying "I'm not a hugger" or "Please don't touch my hair/belly/shoulder."
- **Rest:** Acknowledging that your body requires sleep and food. When you are hungry or tired, you are allowed to stop.
- **Safety:** Removing yourself immediately from any situation where you feel physically threatened or unsafe.

Example: You are at a family gathering and a relative keeps poking you or grabbing your arm while talking. A physical boundary sounds like: *"I love talking to you, but please don't grab my arm. It hurts."*

2. Emotional Boundaries (Your Feelings) This is the fence that prevents you from becoming an emotional sponge. It separates your emotions from the emotions of others.

- **Not Absorbing:** Just because your spouse is in a bad mood does not mean you have to be in a bad mood. You can be compassionate without being infected.
- **Not Fixing:** Accepting that others are allowed to be sad, angry, or disappointed, and it is not your job to "cheer them up" immediately.
- **Name-Calling/Respect:** Refusing to accept shaming or abusive language.

Example: Your partner comes home angry about work and starts venting at you. An emotional boundary sounds like: *"I can see you had a terrible day, and I want to hear about it. But I need you to speak to me calmly. If you keep yelling, I'm going to go into the other room until we can talk respectfully."*

3. Time and Energy Boundaries (Your Resources) This is your calendar and your capacity. It acknowledges that you are finite.

- **Availability:** Deciding when you answer your phone and when you don't.
- **Lateness:** Deciding how long you will wait for someone who is chronically late.
- **Favors:** Deciding how much you can volunteer or help without resentment.

Example: A friend asks you to help them move on Saturday, but you are exhausted from the week. A time boundary sounds like: *"I'd love to help you celebrate once you're settled, but I'm not available to help with the heavy lifting this weekend."*

4. Mental Boundaries (Your Thoughts) This is one we often forget in Christian circles, where groupthink can be strong. A mental boundary protects your right to have your own thoughts, opinions, and theology.

- **Disagreement:** You can love someone and disagree with their politics, their parenting style, or their interpretation of Scripture.
- **Listening:** You can listen to someone's opinion without adopting it as your own.
- **Respect:** You allow others to be wrong (in your eyes) without needing to correct them or convince them.

Example: Your parent starts criticizing your choice of church. A mental boundary sounds like: *"I know we see this differently, and I respect your view. However, I'm really happy where we are worshiping, and I'm not open to debating it right now."*

PRACTICAL APPLICATION: INSTALLING THE GATE

Knowing what a boundary is doesn't make it easy to set one.

When you first start installing these gates, you are going to feel like a mean construction worker. You are going to feel like you are putting up "Keep Out" signs all over your life.

This is normal.

If people are used to walking through your yard whenever they want, they are going to be confused when they hit a fence. They might rattle the gate. They might yell over the fence, "Hey! What is this doing here? I liked the shortcut!"

This brings us back to the most important tool we discussed in Chapter 5: The Internal Pause.

Before you say "Yes" or "No," before you open the gate, you check the latch.

The Gate-Check Questions:

1. **Whose yard is this?** (Is this my problem to solve, or theirs?)
2. **Do I have resources in my shed?** (Do I have the energy/time/money to help right now?)
3. **Is it safe to open the gate?** (Is this person respectful, or will they trample my flowers?)

If the answer is "This is their yard," "My shed is empty," or "They are not safe," keep the gate closed.

This is not cruelty. It is stewardship.

Imagine if the White House had no fence. Imagine if anyone could walk into the Oval Office during a crisis meeting. It would be chaos. The President couldn't do his job.

You have a job to do. You have a life to live, a God to serve, and people to love. You cannot do that work if your office is a public thoroughfare.

WHY THE GATE IS THE MOST LOVING CHOICE

I want you to really hear this: **The person with the strongest boundaries is often the most loving person in the room.**

Why? Because they are not resentful.

When you know you have a gate, when you know you can close it if you need to, you feel safe enough to leave it open when you want to.

The Rigid person keeps the gate locked because they are afraid. The Porous person has no gate because they are afraid. The Healthy person operates the gate with confidence.

Because Mark set a boundary with Steve, Mark didn't burn out. He didn't quit his job. He didn't scream at Steve in the breakroom three months later. He preserved the professional relationship by putting limits on it.

Boundaries protect the connection. They clear out the weeds of resentment so that the flowers of love can actually grow.

You are building a garden where love can be sustained. And for that, you need a gate.

The Internal Gatekeeper: Why You Are Your Own Worst Trespasser

We have spent a lot of time talking about neighbors who trample your grass, friends who demand too much time, and family members who overstep. It is easy to look at boundaries as a tool to manage "difficult people."

But if we are going to be honest, "2:00 AM honest", we have to admit that the person who violates your boundaries the most is often... you.

You are the one who promised yourself you'd get eight hours of sleep, but then you stayed up until midnight doomscrolling news that made you anxious. You are the one who promised yourself you wouldn't check work emails on the weekend, but then you "just took a peek" on Saturday morning and ruined your mood. You are the one who promised to speak kindly to yourself, but then spent your entire commute berating yourself for a minor mistake.

We often think of a boundary as a fence that keeps *others* out. But a boundary is also a leash that keeps *you* in.

In the New Testament, one of the fruits of the Spirit is *self-control* (Galatians 5:23). The Greek word is *egkrateia*, which literally means "mastery from within." It is the ability to hold oneself in check.

If you build a ten-foot wall to keep your mother-in-law from stressing you out, but you spend three hours a day terrorizing yourself with negative self-talk, you are not safe. You have just locked yourself in a room with a bully.

We need to install an **Internal Gatekeeper**.

THE TODDLER AND THE PARENT

To understand internal boundaries, you have to realize that you are two people.

1. **The Toddler:** This is your impulsive, tired, or anxious self. The Toddler wants what feels good *now*. The Toddler wants to eat the whole bag of chips, procrastinate the hard conversation, and scroll TikTok until their eyes burn to avoid feeling lonely.
2. **The Parent:** This is your wise, Spirit-led self. The Parent knows what you need for the long haul. The Parent knows you need sleep, nutrition, prayer, and rest.

When we lack internal boundaries, we let the Toddler run the house. We let our impulses drive the car. And just like a house run by a toddler, our lives become chaotic, sticky, and exhausted.

Setting an internal boundary is simply the Wise Parent stepping in to say, *"I love you too much to let you do this to yourself."*

Here are the three specific zones where your Internal Gatekeeper needs to be on high alert.

Zone 1: The Digital Boundary (Numbing vs. Resting)

For the anxious heart, the phone is a pacifier. When we feel overwhelmed, lonely, or bored, we instinctively reach for the screen. We call it "relaxing," but it is actually "numbing." Relaxing restores you. Numbing depletes you. You know the difference by how you feel afterward. After a nap (relaxing), you feel refreshed. After an hour of scrolling Instagram (numbing), you feel drained, envious, and scattered.

The Internal Boundary: You have to set a limit on your own consumption. Not because technology is evil, but because you are finite.

- *The Rule:* "I do not bring my phone into the bedroom."
- *The Why:* "Because I value my sleep more than I value being entertained."
- *The Gatekeeper Script:* When the Toddler reaches for the phone at 10:00 PM, the Wise Parent says: *"No. We are closing the shop. Put it in the kitchen. Go to sleep."*

Zone 2: The Rumination Boundary (The Worry Loop)

We often think of thoughts as things that "just happen" to us, like weather. But Scripture tells us to "take captive every thought" (2 Corinthians 10:5). This means we have the authority to set boundaries on our own brain. If you have an anxious attachment style, your brain loves to ruminate. It loves to replay a conversation from three days ago, analyzing every tone of voice to see if you were rejected. It loves to write tragedy scripts about the future.

The Internal Boundary: You are allowed to tell your brain, *"We are not doing this right now."* When you catch yourself spiraling into a "What if?" loop at 2:00 AM, you treat the thought like an unsolicited salesperson at the door.

- *The Rule:* "I do not problem-solve after 9:00 PM."
- *The Gatekeeper Script:* *"I hear you, Anxiety. I know you're trying to protect me. But I am not opening the door to this worry right now. If it's important, we can talk about it tomorrow at 10:00 AM. Right now, the gate is closed."*

Zone 3: The Integrity Boundary (Keeping Promises to Yourself)

This is the most painful one. How many times have you broken a promise to yourself that you would never break to a friend? If you promised a friend you'd meet them for a walk, you show up. But if you promised yourself you'd go for a walk, you easily blow it off to finish "one more email." Every time you break a promise to yourself, you damage your self-trust. You teach your internal nervous system: *"I don't matter. My needs are negotiable."*

The Internal Boundary: You must start treating your appointments with yourself as sacred.

- *The Rule:* "If I put it on the calendar, I honor it."
- *The Gatekeeper Script:* When the urge comes to skip your workout to help a colleague, the Wise Parent says: *"No. I promised myself I would move my body today. I keep my promises to me."*

THE THEOLOGY OF SELF-CONTROL

I want to be clear: This is not about "hustle" or "willpower." This is about stewardship. In 1 Corinthians 9:27, Paul says, "I strike a blow to my body and make it my slave so that after I have preached to others, I myself will not be disqualified for the prize." That sounds harsh, but the Greek implies training an athlete. Paul is saying, *"I am the boss of my impulses. I don't let my temporary desires ruin my ultimate calling."*

When you set an internal boundary, when you close the laptop, put down the phone, or refuse to engage in self-pity, you are not restricting your freedom. You are protecting your purpose. You are ensuring that the vessel God wants to use isn't cracked, leaked, or clogged with junk.

So, as you build your fences for the neighbors, don't forget to lock the fridge, silence the phone, and tuck yourself in on time. You are the Gatekeeper. Be a good one.

THE BOUNDARY BUILDER: IDENTIFYING YOUR STYLE

Let's get honest. We all tend toward one style or another, and it often changes depending on the relationship. You might be a Fortress at work, but a Doormat with your mother.

Take a moment to audit three key areas of your life.

1. Work / Service:

- **My Style:** (Porous, Rigid, or Healthy?)
- **Symptom:** Do you say yes to every project? Do you resent your boss? Or do you wall off and refuse to help anyone?

2. Extended Family:

- **My Style:** (Porous, Rigid, or Healthy?)
- **Symptom:** Do you absorb your parents' guilt? Do you dread holidays? Or have you cut everyone off because it's "too much drama"?

3. Primary Relationship (Spouse, Partner, or Closest Friend):

- **My Style:** (Porous, Rigid, or Healthy?)
- **Symptom:** Do you feel responsible for their moods? Do you hide your true feelings to keep the peace?

Write it down. Don't judge it. Just notice where the fences are missing, and where the walls might be too high.

In the next chapter, we're going to talk about the specific words to use when you're standing at that gate, hand on the latch, feeling your throat tighten, trying to figure out how to say "No" without sounding like a jerk.

You have the structure. Now, let's give you the scripts.

8

SCRIPTS FOR REAL LIFE: WHAT TO SAY WHEN IT MATTERS MOST

K nowing you need a boundary and actually saying it are two very different things.

In the quiet of your own mind, or while reading a book like this, boundaries make perfect sense. You can logically agree, "Yes, I need to stop volunteering for everything," or "Yes, I need to tell my brother I can't loan him money again."

But then, reality happens.

You are standing in the church lobby, holding a lukewarm coffee, and the Children's Ministry Director corners you. She looks exhausted. She says, "We are desperate for a nursery volunteer next month. I know you're great with kids. Can we count on you?"

Your brain knows the answer is no. You are already burnt out. You promised your spouse you would slow down.

But your mouth betrays you.

"Sure! I think I can make that work."

As you walk away, a wave of **heavy dread** washes over you. *Why did I* *say that?* you think. *I didn't mean that.* Now I have to go home and tell my husband I failed again.

I call this "The Freeze."

It is a physiological response. When we are put on the spot, especially by someone we want to please or someone who holds authority, our nervous system perceives the moment as a threat. The fear of disappointing them, the fear of their anger, or the fear of awkward silence sends our brain into survival mode.

And for those of us with a history of people-pleasing or anxious attachment, survival mode looks like Appeasement. We feel a sudden **numbness**, or our shoulders slump in defeat, and we say "yes" to lower the immediate tension, even if it creates long-term chaos.

This chapter is your override switch.

We are going to move from the theory of boundaries to the practice of them. I am going to give you specific scripts, words you can memorize, write on sticky notes, or keep in the notes app on your phone.

Some people tell me, "But using a script feels fake. It feels robotic."

Think of these scripts like training wheels. When you are learning to ride a bike, you need the extra support to keep you upright. You aren't going to use training wheels forever. Eventually, your balance will kick in, and you will ride freely. But right now, while your "boundary muscles" are shaky, you need prepared language to keep you from crashing.

Scripture tells us, "Let your 'Yes' be 'Yes,' and your 'No,' be 'No'" (Matthew 5:37).

This is a call to simplicity. It is a call to integrity. But getting there requires practice.

Let's put the training wheels on.

THE CORE FORMULA: CLEAR, KIND, BRIEF

Before we get to the specific scenarios, we need to understand the anatomy of a healthy boundary script.

Most of us, when we try to say no, fall into a trap I call **The Anxious Ramble**. It usually sounds something like this:

"Oh, gosh, I am so sorry, I would really love to help, honestly I would, but things have just been so crazy lately with the kids and work, and my husband really wants me to be home more, and my back has been hurting, so I don't think I can right now, but maybe ask me next month? I feel terrible!"

Do you see what happened there?

1. You apologized for having a limit.
2. You over-explained (JADE).
3. You left the door open for negotiation.

When we are anxious, we instinctively try to soften the blow by offering a mountain of reasons. We think if we provide enough evidence for why we are saying no, the other person won't be mad.

But here is the hard truth: **Over-explaining is a trauma response.**

In the recovery world, there is an acronym called JADE: Justify, Argue, Defend, Explain.

When you JADE, you are subconsciously handing the other person the authority to judge whether your excuse is "good enough." You are inviting them to solve your problem so you can say yes.

If you say, "I can't because I don't have a babysitter," you have just invited them to say, "No problem! You can bring the kids!" Now you are trapped.

We need to replace The Anxious Ramble with **The Secure Statement**.

The Secure Statement has three parts:

1. **Affirmation (Optional):** A brief kindness to connect with the person.
2. **The Limit:** The clear "No" or decision.
3. **Release:** Letting go of the outcome without over-explaining.

It looks like this: *"Thank you for thinking of me (Affirmation). I'm not available to serve in the nursery this season (The Limit). I hope you find the right person (Release)."*

Notice the difference? It is clear. It is kind. And it is brief.

Clear is Kind. Ambiguity is what causes confusion and resentment. When you are brief, you protect your own peace, and you respect the other person's intelligence.

A Note on Delivery: Stop the Nervous Laughter

Before we practice the words, we have to talk about the delivery. You can say the perfect script, but if you say it with a giggle, a wince, or a question mark at the end, you sabotage the boundary.

Many of us have a habit of nervous laughter. We say, "No, I can't do that, haha!"

That little laugh is a signal. It tells the other person, *I'm uncomfortable, I'm not serious, please push me.*

When you practice these scripts, I want you to practice dropping your voice at the end of the sentence. A statement goes down. A question goes up.

- **Weak:** "I don't think I can come?" (Voice goes up).
- **Strong:** "I won't be able to make it." (Voice goes down).

You do not need to be mean. You do not need to be loud. You just need to be steady.

Category 1: The "Delay" Scripts (Buying Time)

The most dangerous moment for a people-pleaser is the ambush, the moment someone asks for a favor face-to-face or on a live phone call.

The pressure to answer now is intense. Your internal monologue is screaming: *If I hesitate, they'll think I'm selfish. If I wait, they'll find someone else. I need to fix this.*

Your goal in this moment is not to give an answer. **Your goal is to buy time.**

You need to get out of the high-pressure environment so you can check in with the Holy Spirit and your own capacity.

The Strategy: Do not say Yes or No. Say "Not yet."

Here is Script Option One, which I call The Capacity Check. "That sounds like a great project. I make it a policy to check my calendar and my capacity before committing to anything new. I will get back to you by [Day]."

Script Option 2 is The Spouse/Partner Buffer. "I've promised [my spouse/family] that I won't agree to new commitments without discussing it with them first. I'll let you know tomorrow."

Script Option 3 is The Vague Hold (For Acquaintances). "Let me think about that and get back to you."

Why this works: These scripts stop the momentum. They break the expectation of instant accessibility. When you say, "I have a policy," you sound professional and wise, not flaky. You are teaching people that your "Yes" is valuable because it is considered, not impulsive.

Category 2: The "Hard No" Scripts (Declining Requests)

Eventually, you have to give the answer. And sometimes, the answer is No.

This is where the fear of rejection spikes. We worry that "No" sounds harsh. But remember: You are not rejecting the person; you are declining the request.

Here are scripts for common scenarios, including three "High-Friction" areas where guilt usually takes over.

Let's look at Scenario A: The Church Volunteer Press (Service Guilt)

The Situation: You are asked to lead a committee or serve in a ministry you are too burnt out to handle. **The Internal Monologue:** *Service is good. If I say no, I'm being lazy. A good Christian would make it work.* **The New Truth:** My first ministry is my own walk with God and my family. Serving out of bitterness honors no one.

The Script: "I love this ministry, but I cannot serve with a cheerful heart in this season because I am at capacity. I'm going to honor God by declining rather than serving out of obligation."

Scenario B: The Social Obligation (The Invitation)

The Situation: You are invited to a baby shower or dinner you do not have the energy to attend. **The Internal Monologue:** *I have to go. It would be rude not to.* **The New Truth:** An invitation is a request, not a subpoena.

Soft (Affirming): "Thank you so much for including me! I won't be able to make it, but I'm so excited for you. I'll be sending a gift along!" **Firm (No excuses):** "I won't be able to join you this time, but have a wonderful time!"

Scenario C: The "Pick Your Brain" Request (The Vague Ask)

The Situation: An acquaintance wants to "grab coffee" to ask for professional advice for free. **The Internal Monologue:** *It's just coffee. I should be helpful.* **The New Truth:** Undefined meetings are energy leaks.

The Script: "I'm heads-down on a few projects right now and not doing coffee meetings, but feel free to send me your specific questions via email, and I'll do my best to answer!"

Scenario D: The Financial or "Favor" Request

The Situation: A sibling or friend asks to borrow money (again). **The Internal Monologue:** *He's family. If I don't help, he might spiral.* **The New Truth:** Enabling incompetence is not love.

You can say: "I love you, and I want to support you, but I'm not lending money to family/friends anymore. It puts too much strain on the relationship, and our relationship is too important to me to risk."

Scenario E: The Parental Sacrifice Card

The Situation: A parent uses their past sacrifices to guilt you into compliance. **The Internal Monologue:** *They gave up everything for me. I owe them this.* **The New Truth:** Love is a gift, not a loan. I cannot repay my parents by erasing my own identity.

The Script: "Mom/Dad, I am so grateful for everything you've done for me. But I cannot pay you back by erasing my own limits. I love you, but the answer to this request is still no."

Scenario F: The "Biblical Peacekeeper" Trap

The Situation: Someone urges you to "just forgive and move on" to avoid conflict, even though the issue isn't resolved. **The Internal Monologue:** *Blessed are the peacemakers. I shouldn't cause trouble.* **The

New Truth: True peace requires truth. Avoiding conflict is just "peace-faking."

The Script: "I am pursuing peace, but peace isn't the same as pretending. I need to resolve the issue before I can 'move on.' Ignoring it isn't peacemaking; it's peace-faking."

Category 3: The "Broken Record" (Handling Pushback)

If everyone accepted our boundaries the first time, you wouldn't need this book. The reality is, people will push back. Especially if they are used to you saying yes.

They might say: "Oh, come on, just this once!" "I thought we were friends." "You're being really rigid."

When this happens, you will feel a desperate urge to JADE. You will want to say, "No, no, let me explain why I can't..."

Do not do this.

When you start explaining your "No" to someone who is pushing, you are handing them a pry-bar to open your boundary.

Instead, use **The Broken Record Technique**.

This technique is simple: You acknowledge their feelings, then you repeat your limit using the exact same words. You do not add new reasons. You just hold the line.

Example Conversation: Friend: "Can you watch my dog this weekend? I know it's last-minute." **You:** "I love Buster, but I'm not able to watch him this weekend." **Friend:** "But I have nowhere else to go! I'm really in a bind. Can't you just make it work?" **You (The Broken Record):** "I know it's stressful to be in a bind. I'm simply not able to watch him this weekend." **Friend:** "Seriously? That really puts me in a tough spot." **You (The Broken Record):** "I hear that you're frustrated. I'm still not able to do it."

Notice what you didn't do. You didn't say, "Well, I have a headache, and my house is messy." By staying with "I am not able," you close the door to negotiation.

Category 4: The "Ending the Conversation" Scripts

Sometimes, a boundary isn't about saying "No" to a task. It's about saying "No" to a way of relating.

If you are in a relationship with someone who is toxic, abusive, or simply refuses to hear you, you need a script to exit the interaction safely.

Script 1: The Anti-Abuse Limit: "I am not willing to be spoken to this way. I am going to [leave the room/hang up] now. We can try again when we can speak calmly."

Script 2: The Circular Argument Stopper: "I've already given you my answer. I'm not going to discuss this further. I'm going to change the subject now."

Script 3: The "Not My Emergency" Script: "I can see you are very upset, and I care about you. However, I cannot fix this for you. I'm going to step away so you can figure out your next steps."

Important Note: When you use these scripts, you must follow through. Words without action are just complaints. Action makes it a boundary.

DIGITAL BOUNDARIES: THE TEXT MESSAGE TRAP

We cannot talk about scripts without talking about the phone in your pocket. For many of us, the hardest boundaries are digital.

Texting creates a false sense of urgency. But a text message is like someone throwing a ball at your head when you aren't looking. You do not have to catch it every time.

Script for the "Immediate Response" Pressure: "I'm stepping away from my phone for the evening/weekend. I'll get back to you when I'm back online."

Script for the Heavy Text Dump: "I want to give this the attention it deserves, and I can't do that over text. Let's find a time to talk about this later in the week."

Script for the Group Chat Overload: "I'm quieting my notifications for a while to focus on some things. If there's an emergency, please call."

Silence as a Boundary

We live in a world that demands attention 24 hours a day. Because of this, many of us have adopted the false belief that Silence = Ignorance or Cruelty.

You do not owe everyone a response.

Silence for Sanity is protective. It is used to regulate your own nervous system and prevent further harm. It says, "This interaction is not healthy, so I am stepping back to keep my peace."

Script for delayed response: "I saw your text. I need some time to process it. I will circle back when I'm ready."

Or, simply... nothing. Jesus did not answer every question the Pharisees asked Him. He often remained silent when the questions were traps. You are allowed to do the same.

Conclusion: The "Script" Becomes Your Voice

I know that reading these scripts might make your **stomach turn**. You might be looking at the "Parental Sacrifice" script and thinking, *I could never say that.*

That is okay. Start small. Start with the barista who gets your order wrong. Start with the acquaintance who asks for coffee when you're busy.

Pick one script from this chapter. Just one. Write it on a sticky note and put it on your bathroom mirror. Practice saying it out loud while you brush your teeth.

"I'm not able to do that." "I'm not able to do that."

It will feel foreign at first. It will feel like you are speaking a different language. In a way, you are. You are speaking the language of self-respect.

But here is the promise: The more you use these scripts, the less you will need them. Eventually, the training wheels will fall off. You won't be reciting a line from a book; you will just be speaking the truth.

You will find that you can say "No" without your voice shaking. You will find that you can withstand someone else's disappointment without crumbling.

And in that clarity, you will find the peace you have been looking for.

The Boundary Builder

Choose Your Weapon: Look back through this chapter. Which scenario made your **shoulders tense up** the most? That is the area where you need the most protection.

1. **Identify the relationship:** (e.g., My boss, my sister, my friend).

2. **Choose the script:** Select one specific sentence from this chapter that applies.
3. **Edit it:** Tweak the words slightly so they sound like you, but do not add JADE (Justify, Argue, Defend, Explain).
4. **Rehearse it:** Say it out loud three times.

You are ready. You are equipped. Let's keep going.

9

BOUNDARIES IN CLOSE RELATIONSHIPS: WHEN IT MATTERS MOST

We have spent the last few chapters in the training dojo. We've dismantled the myths that make boundaries feel unloving. We've practiced the scripts. We've learned the "pause." You probably feel a little stronger, a little clearer, and maybe even ready to try out a "No" on the PTA president or the neighbor who keeps asking to borrow your lawnmower.

But now, we have to leave the safety of the dojo and step into the arena.

If life were a video game, this chapter would be the "Final Boss" level. It is one thing to set a boundary with a stranger or a coworker; it is an entirely different thing to set a boundary with the people who hold your heart.

When you say "no" to an acquaintance, the worst that usually happens is a moment of awkward social tension. But when you say "no" to a spouse, a parent, or a lifelong friend, the stakes feel infinitely higher. These are the relationships that form the scaffolding of your life. The fear isn't just awkwardness; it's loss.

- If I stop fixing my husband's problems, will he pull away?

- If I tell my mother I can't come for Christmas, will I break her heart?
- If I stop being the "available one" for my friends, will they stop calling?

I want you to know right now: This fear is valid. You aren't crazy for feeling it, and you aren't "weak" for hesitating. You are disrupting established contracts, unspoken agreements that have likely been in place for years, perhaps even decades. You are changing the dance steps in the middle of a tango, and yes, people are going to stumble.

But here is the truth we are going to hold onto in this chapter, the anchor in the storm: **You cannot build a truthful relationship on a foundation of pretense.**

If you are only loved because you are compliant, you aren't being loved; you are being used. If the relationship can only survive as long as you are exhausted, it isn't a relationship; it's a hostage situation.

We are going to walk through the four hardest rooms in your life, Marriage, Family, Friendship, and Church, and look at what it means to love securely in each one. We will look at the specific fears that arise, the scripts to use, and how to handle the inevitable "change back" pressure.

SECTION 1: THE MARRIAGE AND PARTNERSHIP

Let's start with the one that often carries the most terror: the person you wake up next to.

For many Christians, the concept of "oneness" in marriage has been weaponized against boundaries. We hear "two shall become one flesh" (Genesis 2:24) and interpret it to mean "two shall become one enmeshed nervous system." We believe that to be a "good" spouse, we must be endlessly available, absorbing our partner's moods, managing their emotions, and anticipating their needs before they even speak them.

But theology and psychology agree on this: **You cannot have oneness if there are not two distinct people.**

Think about the Trinity. Father, Son, and Holy Spirit are perfectly one, yet they are distinct persons. They are not a blur. They have distinct roles and distinct wills that move in perfect harmony.

If I pour a glass of water into a glass of wine, I don't get a union; I get diluted wine. For a marriage to be healthy, there must be a "Me," a "You," and a "We." Boundaries are the lines that keep the "Me" and "You" distinct so that the "We" can be strong.

The Fear: Boundaries = Divorce

The biggest barrier to setting boundaries in marriage is the catastrophic thought: *If I draw a line, I am starting the path to divorce.*

We often view boundaries as walls. We think, *If I put up a wall, I am shutting my spouse out.* But in a healthy marriage, boundaries are not walls of rejection; they are definitions of responsibility. They are the guardrails that keep the relationship from driving off a cliff.

When you lack boundaries, resentment builds. Resentment is actually a much faster path to divorce than boundaries are. Boundaries prevent the burnout that leads to checking out.

Case Study: The "Good Husband" Trap

Let's look at a scenario that challenges the stereotype that only women struggle with this.

Meet Mark. Mark is a gentle soul, a deacon at his church, and a man who loves his wife, Rachel, deeply. Rachel struggles with high anxiety and a sharp tongue when she's stressed.

For ten years, Mark's strategy was "Peace at Any Cost." When Rachel came home from work in a spiral of negativity, Mark would drop everything to soothe her. When she criticized his driving or his cooking, he would apologize just to make the tension stop. He absorbed her stress like a sponge.

Mark told himself he was being a servant-leader. He told himself he was "laying down his life" as Christ did for the church. But internally? Mark was exhausted. He had begun to dread the sound of the garage door opening. He found himself staying late at work just to avoid the emotional minefield at home.

His internal monologue was a constant battle: *I just want her to be happy. If I can just fix this, we'll have a good evening. Why am I so heavy? I must be a bad husband if I feel this drained.*

His lack of boundaries wasn't saving his marriage; it was slowly suffocating his love. He was disappearing.

One Tuesday, after reading about the "Separate Self," Mark tried something new. Rachel came home and immediately started venting about the messy kitchen, her voice rising, her energy chaotic, accusing him of not caring about the house.

Usually, Mark would rush to clean, apologize, and soothe. This time, he paused.

He didn't feel a racing heart; he felt a familiar, crushing heaviness. A wave of numbness washed over him, urging him to just go limp, apologize, and agree, anything to make the conflict disappear. It was the classic "Fawn" response. The dread felt like a physical weight pressing him into the floor.

But he kept his feet planted. He looked at her and said, "I can see you're really overwhelmed, and I want to hear about your day. But I can't engage when you're speaking to me with that tone. I'm going to go to the bedroom for twenty minutes. When you're ready to talk calmly, I'll be there."

He walked away.

Mark sat on the edge of the bed, feeling weak and heavy. He thought, *I've done it. She's going to explode. This is the end.*

Rachel was shocked. She was angry. She banged a few cabinet doors. But twenty minutes later, the house was quiet. She knocked on the bedroom door. Her voice was lower. "I'm sorry," she said. "I had a terrible day, and I took it out on you."

Mark didn't divorce her. He didn't stop loving her. He just refused to be the dumping ground for her dysregulation. By setting a boundary, he invited her to rise to a healthier level of communication. He treated her like an adult who could manage her own emotions, rather than a child who needed him to fix them.

Practical Application: Where to Draw the Line

In marriage, boundaries often look less like grand declarations and more like small pivots in behavior.

1. Emotional Dumping vs. Venting There is a difference between a partner sharing their burdens (which is intimacy) and a partner dumping their toxic stress onto you (which is abuse of the relationship). Venting has a purpose; dumping is just a release of pressure at your expense.

- **Script:** "I love you, and I want to support you, but I don't have the emotional capacity to process this right now. Can we talk about it after dinner when I can actually listen?"
- **Script for the "Fixer":** "I realized I've been trying to solve this for you, and that's not fair to either of us. I trust you to handle this situation at work, but I'm here to give you a hug."

2. The Timing of Conflict You are allowed to not fight at 11:00 PM. Nothing good happens in a marital conversation after everyone is exhausted.

- **Script:** "I'm too tired to have a productive conversation, and I don't want to say something I regret. Let's pause this until Saturday morning when we have coffee."

Note: Always offer a "return time." Walking away without a return time triggers abandonment fears. Saying "Let's talk Saturday" creates safety.

3. Personal Space "Oneness" does not mean you lose the right to solitude. You are allowed to have hobbies, friends, and time alone.

- **Script:** "I need an hour of alone time to recharge so I can be present with you later. I'm going for a walk."

SECTION 2: THE FAMILY OF ORIGIN

If marriage is the hardest room, the Family of Origin is the oldest room. It's the room where your programming was installed. It is where you learned what "love" feels like.

This is where we run headfirst into the "Honor Your Father and Mother" guilt trap. We worry that if we set limits with our parents, we are violating the Ten Commandments.

But we must distinguish between honoring and obeying. **Obedience** is for children. It is a temporary developmental stage. **Honor** is for adults. It means treating them with dignity, respect, and care.

You can honor your parents while disagreeing with them. You can honor them while refusing to participate in unhealthy dynamics. In fact, sometimes the most honoring thing you can do is refuse to enable their sin or dysfunction.

Genesis establishes a principle that supersedes the childhood command to obey: *"Therefore a man shall leave his father and his mother and hold fast to his wife"* (Genesis 2:24).

This "leaving and cleaving" isn't just about geography. You can live three thousand miles away and still be emotionally enmeshed. Leaving means your primary loyalty, your primary validation, and your primary decision-making center shifts from them to you (and your new family, if you have one).

Case Study: The Holiday Hostage

Let's look at the classic "Holiday Guilt" scenario.

Jessica's mother, Brenda, loves Christmas. And by "loves," I mean she expects all three of her adult children to be at her house from Christmas Eve until Boxing Day, sleeping in their childhood twin beds, following her schedule, and eating her food.

Jessica is now 35, married, and has a toddler. The travel is exhausting. She wants to start her own traditions. She wants to wake up in her own house on Christmas morning and watch her son open presents without having to pack a suitcase immediately after.

Every time Jessica hints at this, Brenda sighs, that heavy, martyred sigh. "Well, I guess I just won't see my grandbaby. It's fine. I'll just be here alone. I worked so hard to make this magical for you, but I guess it doesn't matter."

Jessica's stomach drops. The "Bad Daughter" alarm blares. She feels the heavy slump of guilt, a desire to just cancel her plans and surrender to avoid hurting her mother.

But this year, Jessica prepares. She sends an email in October (proactive boundaries are always better than reactive ones).

> *"Mom, we love you and can't wait to celebrate with you. This year, we are going to do Christmas morning at our own house to start some new traditions for Leo. We will be there for dinner on Christmas Eve and would love to see you the weekend after."*

Brenda calls, crying. She uses the Guilt Weapon. She uses the "You've changed" weapon. *"I don't even know who you are anymore. Your husband is pulling you away from us."*

This is the moment of truth.

Jessica holds the line. She uses the "Broken Record" technique from Chapter 8. She doesn't JADE (Justify, Argue, Defend, Explain).

"I know it's different, and I know you're disappointed. We love you, and this is what works for our family this year."

She doesn't apologize for growing up. She acknowledges her mother's feelings ("I know you're disappointed") without taking responsibility for fixing them.

Managing the "You've Changed" Accusation

When you start setting boundaries with family, they will likely say, "You've changed." They say it like an accusation, like a verdict of guilt.

I want you to receive it as a compliment.

You *have* changed. You have stopped being a child who is afraid of conflict and started being an adult who values truth. You have stopped playing a role in a script you didn't write.

- **Script for the Guilt Trip:** "I know this is disappointing. I'm not trying to hurt you; I'm trying to take care of my health/family. I hope you can understand."
- **Script for Unsolicited Parenting Advice:** "I appreciate that you care about how we raise the kids, Mom, but we've made our decision on this." (Repeat as necessary).
- **Script for Gossip:** If your parent tries to talk to you about your sibling: "I'm not comfortable talking about [Sibling] when they aren't here. Let's talk about something else. How is your garden?"

What if They Cut Me Off?

This is the dark fear at the bottom of the well. "If I set a boundary, will they stop talking to me?"

In extreme cases of toxicity, yes, a parent might pull away to punish you. This is incredibly painful. But if their love is conditional on your absolute obedience, you never really had the relationship you thought you had. You had a transaction.

Most of the time, however, parents eventually adjust. It takes time. They may pout for a season. They may be cold for a few months. But if you stay steady, warm but firm, they usually realize that if they want a relationship with you, they have to accept the adult version of you.

SECTION 3: FRIENDSHIPS

Friendships are unique because there is no legal contract binding you together. There is no bloodline. There is only the voluntary choice to stay connected. This makes boundaries tricky because we fear that if we stop being "useful," the friendship will evaporate.

Many of us who struggle with anxious attachment have built friendships on a foundation of over-functioning. We are the "Listener." We are the "Rescuer." We are the one who drops everything. We unconsciously believe: *I must be useful to be kept.*

The Concept of Reciprocity

Healthy adult friendship is based on reciprocity. This doesn't mean a perfect 50/50 split every single day; sometimes you are in crisis, sometimes they are. But over the arc of a year, the energy flow should be roughly equal.

If you leave every coffee date feeling drained, used, or invisible, you do not have a friendship. You have a ministry. And you need to know the difference.

Case Study: The Askhole and the Crisis Junkie

We all know an "Askhole." This is the friend who calls you in a panic, asks for your advice for an hour, nods while you pour out your wisdom, and then does exactly what she was going to do anyway. Two weeks later, she calls you with the same problem.

Or perhaps you have the "Crisis Junkie." This friend's life is a perpetual series of emergencies. Every text is in all caps. Every minor inconvenience is a catastrophe.

Your role in these friendships has likely been the "Stabilizer." You listen, you fix, you offer biblical wisdom. You feel important because you are needed. But you are also tired. You realize you haven't shared a struggle of your own in three years because there is never any room for you.

Setting a boundary here means stepping out of the Rescuer role. It means trusting God to be their Savior, so you don't have to apply for the job.

Practical Application: Shifting the Dynamic

1. For the "Askhole": Stop Giving Advice. The next time they present the same problem they have had for five years, do not offer a solution.

- **Script:** "Wow, that sounds really hard. You've been dealing with this for a while. What do you think you're going to do?"

(*Put the ball back in their court. It is not your job to solve a problem they aren't willing to fix. This forces them to engage their own agency.*)

2. For the Crisis Junkie: Limit Your Availability. You are not 911. Unless there is immediate physical danger, you do not need to answer every text instantly.

- **Script:** "I have about 15 minutes to chat, but then I have to go start dinner."
- **Script:** "I'm in a season where I don't have the capacity to process heavy stuff right now. I love you, but I need to keep our convos light for a bit. Can we just talk about movies or books today?"

3. The Fade Sometimes, when you stop over-functioning, the friendship naturally fades. The other person realizes they can't use you anymore, and they drift away. This is painful, but it is also a mercy. It clears the space for friends who want to know you, not just use your ears.

SECTION 4: CHURCH AND MINISTRY

Finally, we step into the sanctuary. This is where boundaries can feel most confusing because we feel we are saying "No" to God.

We face the "Super Christian" pressure, the unspoken belief that if you really loved Jesus, you would teach Sunday School, lead the small group, bake for the potluck, and mentor three teenagers, all with a smile.

We confuse **Service** with **Slavery**.

- **Service** comes from a place of overflow. It is "God has given me so much, I want to pour out."
- **Slavery** (or religious obligation) comes from a place of deficit. It is "I must do this so I am good enough/so they won't judge me/so the church won't collapse."

Remember: Your primary ministry is your own household and your own mental health. You cannot pour from an empty cup, and God gets no glory from your burnout. Jesus himself frequently withdrew from the crowds to pray. He said "No" to needs in one town so he could move to the next. If the Messiah had boundaries, you are allowed to have them too.

The "Messiah Complex" in the Pews

We often think, *If I don't do it, no one will. If I don't run the nursery, it will close. If I don't lead the Bible study, the women won't be fed.*

This is a subtle form of pride. It assumes that God's plan relies entirely on your exhaustion. If you step back, God is big enough to raise up someone else, or perhaps that program needs to end for a season.

Practical Application: Stepping Back Without Shame

You do not owe the church committee an explanation for your "No."

- **Script for Turning Down a Role:** "Thank you so much for thinking of me. I've prayed about it, and I don't have the capacity to serve in that role this season. I'm going to pass."

Note: You didn't say "I'm too busy." If you say you're busy, they will try to problem-solve your schedule ("It's only once a month!"). Just say you don't have the capacity.

- **Script for the "Guilt Trip" from Leadership:** "I know there's a big need, and I trust God will provide the right person. It just isn't me right now."

CONCLUSION: THE NEW CONTRACT

Setting boundaries in these close relationships is terrifying. I won't lie to you.

The first time you do it, your stomach might feel heavy as lead. You might feel a wave of numbness or the urge to just go silent to keep the peace. You might feel the "Fawn" instinct kicking in, that dread that says, *Just agree, just apologize, make it stop.*

You might doubt everything. *Did I just ruin everything? Am I being selfish?*

But as you hold the line, as Mark did with Rachel, as Jessica did with her mom, something miraculous happens.

The relationship changes.

The unspoken contract of "I will disappear so you can be comfortable" is torn up. And a new contract is written: "I will be a whole person, and I invite you to be a whole person, and we will love each other from that place."

Some people won't sign the new contract. That is the risk. Some friends may fall away. Some family members may stay angry. But the ones who do sign it? The ones who respect your "No" and value your voice?

Those are the relationships that will sustain you for a lifetime. Those are the relationships that reflect the Kingdom of God, where love is free, not coerced.

You are doing the hard work. You are fighting for a love that is real, safe, and sustainable.

The Gatekeeper's Truth

> *"Above all else, guard your heart, for everything you do flows from it."*
>
> — PROVERBS 4:23

Reflection: You are not walling people out; you are guarding the sacred space God entrusted to you. When you guard the wellspring of your life, you ensure that the love flowing out of it remains pure, rather than polluted by resentment.

The Boundary Builder

Exercise: The New Contract

This week, identify one relationship where you feel exhausted. Write down the "Unspoken Contract" you have been operating under, and then write the "New Clause" you are enacting.

- **Example (Parent):**
  - *Old Contract:* I will always answer the phone when you call so you don't feel lonely, even if I am working.
  - *New Clause:* I will love you, but I am not responsible for your loneliness. I will call you back when I am free.
- **Example (Spouse):**
  - *Old Contract:* I will absorb your stress so we can have a peaceful evening.
  - *New Clause:* I will be a loving partner, but I will not be the container for your unregulated emotions.

Your Turn:

- **Relationship:** _____
- **Old Contract:** _____
- **New Clause:** _____

10

MANAGING PUSHBACK, GUILT, AND EMOTIONAL FALLOUT

You did it. You finally said the thing.

Maybe you told your mother you aren't coming for Christmas this year. Maybe you told your boss you won't be answering emails after 6:00 p.m. Maybe you finally told that friend who drains you that you can't meet for coffee this week.

You said the words. You held the line. You did exactly what we've been talking about for the last nine chapters.

And now? You feel terrible.

Welcome to the **Vulnerability Hangover**.

If you are anything like the hundreds of people I've walked through this process, right now your brain is probably screaming some variation of: *What have I done? I went too far. I was too harsh. They're going to hate me. I'm a terrible Christian. I need to fix this immediately.*

But pay attention to your body. In the past, we might have called this panic or a racing heart. But for many of us, the reaction to setting a boundary is actually a sudden **heaviness**. Your shoulders slump. A numbness spreads through your chest. You feel a distinct, heavy dread that makes you want to curl up or go silent. This is the "Fawn" response, trying to drag you back into submission.

You check your phone every thirty seconds to see if they've texted, or maybe you've buried your phone under a pillow because you're dreading that they *will* text. You feel a low-level ache to call them back and say, "Just kidding! I didn't mean it! I'll do whatever you want!"

Take a breath. A deep one. In through your nose, hold it for a count of four, and out through your mouth.

Do it again.

Now, hear me when I say this: You are not crazy. You are not unloving. And you have not ruined everything.

What you are feeling right now, this heavy cocktail of dread, guilt, and numbness, is not proof that you made a mistake. It is proof that you disrupted a system. Your nervous system has spent a lifetime equating "keeping the peace" with safety and "disappointing others" with danger. By setting a boundary, you just walked directly into what your body perceives as a threat. Of course, you feel heavy. Of course, you feel the urge to slump.

But feelings are not facts. The dread is real, but the danger is not.

You have stepped into a new way of relating, and your body is simply catching up to your bravery. So before you pick up that phone to undo all your hard work, let's talk about what is actually happening, and why the chaos you're feeling might actually be a sign of health.

THE PHYSIOLOGY OF THE NO: A RECOVERY PROTOCOL

We need to pause here for a moment. I don't want to just give you *theory* about why you feel bad; I want to give you a *protocol* for what to do when your hands are shaking.

Because here is the reality: You cannot "think" your way out of a nervous system reaction.

When you set a hard boundary, especially with a parent or a spouse, your body enters a high-alert state. You have just violated a primal safety rule ("Don't upset the tribe"), and your amygdala is currently dumping cortisol and adrenaline into your bloodstream.

That is why you feel that urge to run, to fix it, or to fawn. That is why your thoughts are racing. Your body is preparing for a tiger attack.

If you try to use logic ("It's okay, I'm an adult, boundaries are healthy") while your body is bracing for impact, the logic won't stick. You have to speak the language of the body first.

I call this the **Boundary Recovery Protocol**. It is a physical first-aid kit for the ten minutes *after* you say the hard thing.

Do not skip this. If you don't discharge this energy, it stays trapped in your body, turning into resentment, migraines, or the sudden urge to eat an entire bag of chips.

Step Number One: The Shake-Out (Discharge the Adrenaline)

Have you ever watched a nature documentary? When a gazelle escapes a cheetah, it doesn't just walk away and start grazing. It stops and *shakes*.

It literally trembles from nose to tail for a few seconds. This is how mammals discharge the massive surge of adrenaline they just used for survival. Once they shake it off, their nervous system resets to "calm," and they go back to eating grass.

Humans are the only mammals who don't do this. We hold it in. We sit frozen on the couch, gripping our phone, holding our breath. We trap the "fight or flight" energy in our muscles.

The Action: Stand up. Right now (or as soon as you are alone). I want you to literally shake your hands, your arms, and your legs. bounce on your heels. Shimmy your shoulders. Do it for 60 seconds. It feels ridiculous. Do it anyway. While you shake, imagine you are physically flicking off the sticky energy of the interaction. You are telling your body, *"The threat is over. We survived. We can let this go."*

Step Number Two: The Physiological Sigh (Reset the Breath)

When we are anxious (or fawning), we tend to shallow-breathe or hold our breath. This signals to the brain: *"We are still in danger."* To flip the switch from Sympathetic (Fight/Flight) to Parasympathetic (Rest/Digest), we need to change the carbon dioxide levels in your blood.

The Action: We are going to use a tool often recommended by neuroscientists called the Physiological Sigh.

1. Inhale deeply through your nose.
2. At the top of the inhale, take one more tiny, sharp inhale through your nose (popping the air sacs in your lungs open).
3. Exhale slowly and fully through your mouth (like you are blowing through a straw) until your lungs are completely empty.
4. Repeat this 3 times.

This is the fastest way to manually override your internal alarm system. It is the "Off" button for the shock collar.

Step 3: Orientation (The "Here and Now" Check)

When you are in a Vulnerability Hangover, your brain is time-traveling. It is likely regressing to a past trauma (being scolded as a child) or catastrophic future (being abandoned forever). You need to bring your brain back to the present moment, where you are safe.

The Action: Look away from your phone. Look away from the person you just spoke to. Find **three rectangular things** in the room. (The window, the book, the rug). Find **two red things**. Find **one thing that**

feels soft. Say them out loud: *"I see the rug. I see the red pillow. I feel the blanket."* This signals to your brain: *"I am here. I am in my living room. There is no tiger. I am an adult woman, and I am safe."*

Step 4: The Truth Anchor (Cognitive Re-framing)

Only *after* you have shaken, breathed, and oriented can you use your words. Now that the noise has dialed down, you can speak truth to your soul. You need a mantra that contradicts the lie of the Fawn Response.

The Action: Place your hand on your chest (this releases oxytocin, the comfort hormone). Say one of these truths out loud:

- *"I am allowed to disappoint people."*
- *"This feeling is not danger; it is just growth."*
- *"I am not harming them; I am protecting us."*
- *"I can handle their displeasure."*

WHY THIS MATTERS FOR YOUR SOUL

You might be thinking, *Is this really spiritual? Shaking my hands?* Yes. Because your body is the temple of the Holy Spirit. And when your temple is flooded with stress hormones because you are trying to be the Savior of your family, you cannot hear the Spirit's voice. Elijah, the great prophet, had a Vulnerability Hangover. After his massive confrontation with the prophets of Baal (a huge boundary-setting moment!), he ran away into the desert and collapsed. He wanted to die. He was depleted. And how did God minister to him? God didn't give him a theology lecture. God gave him a nap and a snack (1 Kings 19). God tended to his body first. So, treat yourself with the same tenderness. Do the protocol. Eat the snack. Take the nap. You are doing heavy lifting. Recovery is part of the work.

The "Change Back" Maneuver

Imagine a mobile hanging above a baby's crib. It's perfectly balanced. The little plastic stars and moons drift peacefully in circles. Now, imagine you reach up and yank on one of the stars. What happens?

The whole thing goes wild. The other pieces swing violently, clattering into each other, spinning out of control. The mobile isn't "broken," but it is definitely disturbed. It will swing chaotically for a while until it finds a new center of gravity.

Relationships are systems, just like that mobile. They rely on homeostasis, a fancy biological term that basically means "staying the same." Systems love stability. They fight to maintain the status quo because the status quo is predictable, and to a survival brain, predictable equals safe.

When you set a boundary, you yanked the star. You disrupted the equilibrium. You stopped playing your assigned part in the script. If your role was "The One Who Always Says Yes" or "The One Who Fixes Everything," and suddenly you stepped off stage, the other actors in your life don't know what to do. They are disoriented. And disoriented people often react with resistance.

This is what family systems theorists call the "Change Back" Maneuver.

When you change, the people around you will often unconsciously (or consciously) pressure you to change back. They want the old you, the one who was convenient, compliant, and predictable. They aren't necessarily villains; they are just humans who have lost their balance.

REALITY CHECK: The "Extinction Burst"

There is a concept in psychology called the "extinction burst." It explains why people often get louder and angrier right before they accept a boundary.

Think of a vending machine. If you put a dollar in and press the button for a Diet Coke, you expect a Diet Coke. If nothing comes out, what do you do? Do you shrug and walk away? No. You press the button again. Harder. You might jiggle the lever. You might kick the machine. You might yell at it.

Your behavior gets louder and more aggressive right before you finally give up.

When you set a boundary, you are essentially unplugging the vending machine. You are no longer dispensing the compliance, validation, or rescue that the other person is used to getting from you. And when they press the button and nothing comes out? They are going to kick the machine.

This escalation is the extinction burst. It is the tantrum of a system fighting to survive. And here is the most important thing you need to know about it: The escalation does not mean your boundary failed. It means your boundary is working.

A Theological Reality Check

I know what you're thinking. *But as a Christian, shouldn't I be bringing peace, not chaos? If people are upset with me, doesn't that mean I'm not reflecting Jesus?*

Let's look at Jesus for a moment.

Did everyone like Jesus? Did everyone feel "at peace" when He was around? Absolutely not. Jesus disrupted systems everywhere He went. He disappointed the Pharisees. He confused His disciples. He upset His own family (remember when they thought He was out of His mind in Mark 3?).

Jesus was the Prince of Peace, yet He said, "Do not suppose that I have come to bring peace to the earth. I did not come to bring peace, but a sword" (Matthew 10:34). He wasn't talking about violence; He was talking about division. He was talking about the inevitable conflict that happens when truth enters a system built on lies, or when health enters a system built on dysfunction.

If Jesus, who was perfect love in human form, disappointed people, caused conflict, and experienced rejection, why do we think we can avoid it?

Persecution or pushback isn't always a sign of sin. Sometimes, it is a sign of health. Sometimes, the anger coming at you is simply the sound of an unhealthy system realizing it can no longer control you.

THE GATEKEEPER'S TRUTH

When the Vulnerability Hangover hits, when that heaviness tries to drag you back into old habits, you need more than just willpower. You need a structural reinforcement. You need **The Gatekeeper's Truth**.

Scripture gives us a blueprint for this in Proverbs:

> *"Like a city whose walls are broken through is a person who lacks self-control."*

> — (PROVERBS 25:28)

For years, your walls have been broken. People wandered in and out, taking your energy and leaving their trash. Now, you are rebuilding the wall. But a wall needs a gate, and a gate needs a Gatekeeper.

When the hangover tells you to apologize or take it back, your inner Gatekeeper must stand firm. Try this **3-Step Gatekeeper Protocol** to combat the dread:

1. **Name the Sensation:** "I am not unsafe; I am just experiencing a Vulnerability Hangover."

2. **Validate the Wall:** "My 'no' was necessary to protect the city of my heart."
3. **Speak the Truth:** "I am rebuilding my walls so I can love from a place of wholeness, not depletion."

DECODING THE PUSHBACK

Once you understand why the pushback is happening, you need to know how to handle it when it shows up at your front door (or in your inbox).

Resistance usually falls into a few predictable categories. I call these the "Four Horsemen of the Boundary Apocalypse." When you can name them, they lose some of their power to overwhelm you.

1. The Guilt Trip ("After All I've Done For You") This is the classic weapon of choice for parents, church leaders, and long-term friends. It leverages your history and your conscience against you. *"I guess I just don't matter to you anymore." "I sacrificed everything for you, and you can't even do this one thing?"*

The Decode: This is a transaction disguised as love. True generosity doesn't keep a ledger. If their "love" comes with a debt repayment plan you never signed up for, it wasn't a gift; it was a loan.

2. The Silent Treatment This is the adult version of holding your breath until you turn blue. It is withdrawal designed to punish. They stop texting. They leave the room when you enter. They give you one-word answers. **The Decode:** Silence is not a boundary; it is manipulation. A boundary says, "I need space to process." The silent treatment says, "I will erase you until you comply."

3. The Rage This is the extinction burst in its purest form. Yelling, accusations, character attacks. *"You are so selfish!" "You've changed. You're arrogant now."*

The Decode: Rage is often a secondary emotion covering up fear. They are terrified of losing control over you, so they get loud to regain dominance. It is the roar of a person who feels their power slipping away.

4. The Victim ("You're Hurting Me") This one is incredibly hard for empathetic Christians. They act crushed. They cry. They talk about how your boundary is damaging their mental health or their heart. *"I can't believe you would treat me this way."*

The Decode: They are confusing hurt with harm. We'll talk more about this in a minute, but remember: you setting a limit on what you will do is not the same as you attacking them.

THE BOUNDARY BUILDER: Do Not JADE

When you are facing any of these reactions, your anxious brain will scream at you to explain yourself. You will want to talk them out of their anger. You will want to make them understand that you really do love them.

You must resist this urge. There is a golden rule for managing push-back: **Do Not JADE.**

J – Justify **A** – Argue **D** – Defend **E** – Explain

When you JADE, you are handing the other person the authority to judge your boundary. You are essentially saying, "Here is my case for why I am allowed to have this need. Please approve it."

But you don't need their approval. This brings us to a vital spiritual principle found in Ephesians 4:25:

"Therefore each of you must put off falsehood and speak truthfully to your neighbor..."

When we JADE, when we offer soft excuses or long explanations to soften the blow, we are often dancing with falsehood. We are trying to control their reaction rather than speaking the plain truth. The "Resentful Yes" is a lie. The "Soft Maybe" when you mean "No" is a lie.

Instead, stand in the truth. Use the scripts we practiced in Chapter 8. Keep it short. Keep it boring.

"I hear that you're upset, but I'm not able to come this year." "I understand you're disappointed. I'm sticking to my decision."

THE INTERNAL BATTLE: MANAGING THE GUILT

The external pushback is hard, but for most of us, the internal battle is worse. You can hang up the phone on a shouting relative, but you can't hang up on your own brain.

Let's talk about guilt.

There are two kinds of guilt: **True Conviction** and **False Guilt**.

True Conviction comes from the Holy Spirit. It happens when you have actually violated a moral law, when you have sinned against God or neighbor. It is specific. It is sharp. And it leads to repentance and restoration. *"I lost my temper and called my husband a name. I need to apologize."*

False Guilt (often called neurotic guilt) comes from your social conditioning and your anxious attachment. It happens when you violate a social expectation or a family rule, not a moral law. It is vague, heavy, and frantic. *"I feel like a bad person because I said no."*

Here is the key distinction you must write on your heart: **Disappointing someone is not the same as harming them.**

Harming someone is sin. It is abuse, neglect, cruelty, or theft. Disappointing someone is simply failing to meet their expectations.

We often confuse being "nice" with being "good." But the Bible warns us about using a veneer of goodness to cover up a lack of integrity. 1 Peter 2:16 says:

"Live as free people, but do not use your freedom as a cover-up for evil; live as God's slaves."

Sometimes, we use our "niceness" as a cover-up for our fear. We call it "service," but it's actually slavery to people-pleasing. True freedom is the ability to say no when necessary, so that your yes is actually holy.

Hannah's Sunday Dinner

Let's look at Hannah. Hannah grew up in a family where Sunday dinner was mandatory. If you missed it, her mother would sigh and say, "It's just sad that family isn't a priority for everyone."

Now, Hannah is 35, married, and has a toddler. Sunday dinners are exhausting. They involve an hour drive each way, a nap-less toddler, and passive-aggressive comments about her parenting. She and her husband are worn out. They are living the reality of Psalm 127:2:

"In vain you rise early and stay up late, toiling for food to eat, for he grants sleep to those he loves."

Hannah realized she was toiling in vain to keep the peace, at the expense of the sleep and rest God wanted to grant her family.

Hannah decides to set a boundary: "We will come for Sunday dinner once a month, but not every week."

Her mother explodes. Then cries. Then goes silent.

Hannah feels sick. She thinks, *I'm breaking the commandment to honor my father and mother. I'm being selfish. Look at how much I've hurt her.*

But let's look closer. Is Hannah harming her mother? Is she stealing from her? Striking her? No. She is restructuring her time to honor her own nuclear family and her need for rest, which is also a biblical command.

Hannah's guilt is a liar. It is telling her she is bad when really she is just separate. She is becoming an adult.

Hannah had to sit with that guilt. She didn't fix it. She didn't call her mom to apologize. She let the guilt scream in the backseat while she drove the car of her life toward health. And you know what? After about three months, the guilt started to get quiet. Her mom stopped throwing tantrums because they stopped working. And Hannah got her Sundays back.

You can hold the line even when you feel terrible. Your feelings do not determine right and wrong. Truth does.

What to Do When They Won't Stop

Sometimes, you do everything right. You use the scripts. You stay calm. You don't, JADE. And they still won't stop.

They show up at your house unannounced. They keep texting after you asked for space. They keep bringing up the topic you said was off-limits.

This is where many people give up. They say, "I set a boundary, but it didn't work."

Here is the hard truth: **A boundary without a consequence is just a suggestion.**

If you tell your toddler, "If you throw that toy, I will take it away," and then they throw the toy, and you do nothing... You have taught them that your words mean nothing. You have taught them that the boundary is actually just a noise you make before you give in.

Adults are the same. If you say, "I will not tolerate being yelled at," but you stay on the phone while they yell, you do not have a boundary. You have a wish.

You must be willing to enforce consequences.

This is not about punishment. Punishment is about making them suffer ("You were mean to me, so now I'm going to be mean to you"). Consequences are about protection ("You are hurting me, so I am removing myself from your reach").

Practical Examples of Consequences:

The Phone Boundary:

- **Boundary:** "Mom, if you continue to criticize my husband, I'm going to get off the phone."
- **Testing:** She continues to criticize him.
- **Consequence:** "Okay, I hear that you want to keep talking about this, so I'm going to go now. I love you. Goodbye." (Click).

The Visit Boundary:

- **Boundary:** "Please call before you come over. If you stop by unannounced, we won't answer the door."
- **Testing:** They knock on the door Saturday morning.
- **Consequence:** You do not open the door. (Yes, this is excruciatingly hard. Yes, they will be mad. Yes, it is necessary.

This is the "Separate Self" in action. You are taking control of the only thing you can control: yourself. You are moving your body, your attention, and your presence away from the violation.

You are teaching people how to treat you. It is a slow, painful training process, but it is the only way to build a relationship based on respect rather than compliance.

Conclusion: The Cost of Peace

I want to end this chapter by talking about peace.

We love the verse, "Blessed are the peacemakers, for they will be called children of God" (Matthew 5:9). But we often confuse peacemaking with peacekeeping.

Peacekeeping is avoiding conflict at all costs. It is sweeping things under the rug. It is a fake peace, a fragile silence that exists only because one person (you) is absorbing all the tension. That is not the peace of God. That is appeasement.

Peacemaking is different. Peacemaking often requires disrupting the false peace to build true peace. It requires entering the conflict, speaking the truth, and doing the hard work of reconciliation, or the hard work of separating when reconciliation isn't possible.

Peacemaking is messy. It is loud. It often feels like war in the beginning.

But it is the only path to a relationship that is real.

You are in the thick of the battle right now. The pushback is hard. The guilt is heavy. But do not mistake the struggle for failure. You are tilling the soil. You are digging up the weeds of dysfunction so that something new can grow.

Hold the line, friend. You are not just fighting for a boundary; you are fighting for the health of your soul and the future of your relationships.

The hangover will pass. The guilt will fade. And on the other side? There is a freedom you haven't even tasted yet.

Keep going.

11

BOUNDARIES, FORGIVENESS, AND GRACE

W e have arrived at the question that weighs heaviest on the hearts of most Christians.

It usually settles in about three weeks after you set a significant boundary. The initial resolve of standing up for yourself has worn off. The spark that fueled your "No" has subsided. The dust has settled.

And now, you are sitting in the quiet, looking at the empty space where that relationship used to be, or looking at the new distance you've created, and a single, heavy thought creeps in:

Am I being unforgiving?

You look at your Bible. You see the verses about "turning the other cheek." You remember Peter asking Jesus how many times he should forgive, and Jesus answering, "Seventy times seven" (Matthew 18:22). You remember the Lord's Prayer: "Forgive us our debts, as we also have forgiven our debtors."

And you feel a cold dread wash over you.

You think *I told my dad he couldn't come over when he's been drinking. I told my friend she couldn't speak to me that way anymore. But if I've really forgiven them, shouldn't things go back to normal?*

If I'm keeping this boundary up, does that mean I'm holding a grudge?

Is my 'No' actually just a lack of grace?

This is the spiritual heavy lifting of boundaries. It is easy to set a limit when we are mad. It is much harder to keep a limit when we feel guilty.

In this chapter, we are going to untangle one of the biggest knots in modern Christian culture: the confusion between **Forgiveness** and **Reconciliation**.

We have been taught that they are the same thing. We have been taught that to forgive someone means to trust them again. We have been taught that "grace" means giving someone the front door key to your life, no matter how many times they have robbed the house.

But that is not what the Bible teaches. And it is certainly not what wisdom teaches.

If you are currently feeling the weight of "spiritual guilt", if you feel like a "bad Christian" because you don't want to let a toxic person back in close, this chapter is for you.

We are going to learn how to forgive fully while keeping the gate locked. We are going to learn how to love from a distance.

The Mathematics of Forgiveness vs. Trust

To understand why we feel so heavy-hearted, we have to look at the "math" we've been taught.

Most of us operate on this equation:

Forgiveness + Time = Restoration

We believe that if we have forgiven someone, and if enough time has passed, the relationship should automatically be restored to its previous state. If it isn't, we assume the failure is on our part. We assume we are "harboring bitterness."

But this equation is missing a variable. The biblical equation looks more like this:

Forgiveness + Repentance + Changed Behavior + Time = Restoration

Do you see the difference? The first equation puts all the work on you. The second equation acknowledges that while forgiveness is a solo act, reconciliation is a partnership.

Let's define our terms, because words matter.

1. Forgiveness (The Debt)

Forgiveness is a **vertical transaction** between you and God. It is the decision to release the other person from the debt they owe you.

When someone hurts you, when they lie, betray, abuse, or neglect you, they steal from you. They steal your peace, your trust, or your dignity. They owe you.

Forgiveness is the legal act of canceling that debt. You say, *"God, I am handing this invoice to You. I am no longer going to try to extract payment from them. I am not going to make them suffer to pay me back. I am letting them off my hook and putting them on Yours."*

You can do this entirely alone. The other person doesn't even need to know. You can forgive a person who is dead. You can forgive a person who isn't sorry. Forgiveness is for your freedom, so you don't carry the poison of bitterness.

2. Reconciliation (The Relationship)

Reconciliation is a **horizontal transaction** between you and the other person. It is the re-establishing of trust.

Trust is not a gift; it is a bank account. It is built through consistent, reliable deposits over time.

If forgiveness is "releasing the debt," reconciliation is "opening a new account."

And here is the hard truth: **You can release the debt without opening a new account.**

If a bank teller steals money from the vault, the bank manager might forgive him. He might decide not to press charges. He might even pray for the man's soul and wish him well. That is forgiveness.

But does the bank manager hire him back the next day and give him the code to the vault?

Absolutely not.

Why? Is the manager holding a grudge? Is he being "unforgiving"?

No. He is being a steward. He knows that the man is not safe to handle money. The debt is gone, but the trust is gone too.

When you set a boundary with someone who has hurt you, you are acting like that bank manager. You are saying, *"I forgive you for what you stole. I am not trying to punish you. But I am not giving you the code to the vault again until you have proven you can be trusted."*

THE "GRUDGE" VS. THE BOUNDARY

So, how do you know the difference in your own heart? How do you know if your "No" is a healthy boundary or a sinful grudge?

I hear this from people all the time: "I feel like I'm punishing my mother by not answering her calls. Isn't that a grudge?"

Let's put them side by side.

The Grudge

A grudge is active. It is hot. It is driven by a desire for the other person to feel pain.

- **The Motive:** Retaliation. "You hurt me, so I want you to feel hurt."
- **The Internal Monologue:** "I hope she suffers. I hope she realizes how much she needs me. I'm going to ignore her so she learns a lesson."
- **The Fruit:** Bitterness, gossip, obsession. You replay the offense over and over. You are tied to them by anger.

The Boundary

A boundary is protective. It can be cool or neutral. It is driven by a desire for safety and health.

- **The Motive:** Preservation. "You hurt me, so I am moving out of range so you cannot hurt me again."
- **The Internal Monologue:** "I wish him well, but I cannot be around him when he is like this. I am staying away to protect my peace."
- **The Fruit:** Grief, perhaps, but ultimately peace. You think about them less. You are free to live your life.

If you are not answering your mother's calls because you want her to sit at home and cry and feel terrible, that is a grudge. Repent of that.

But if you are not answering her calls because every time you speak to her, she is verbally abusive, and it takes you three days to recover your equilibrium, that is a boundary. That is stewardship.

You are not punishing her. You are protecting you.

Case Study: The King and the Cave (David's Boundary)

If you need biblical proof that you can honor someone while refusing to be near them, we need to look at the relationship between David and King Saul.

This is one of the most complex, painful relationships in Scripture. Saul was God's anointed king. He was also David's father-in-law. And he was toxic, abusive, and arguably mentally ill. Saul spent years hunting David down, trying to kill him out of jealousy. David spent years running.

There is a famous scene in 1 Samuel 24. David is hiding in a cave in the wilderness of En Gedi. By chance, Saul comes into that very cave to relieve himself, unaware that David and his men are hiding in the shadows.

David's men whisper, *"This is it! God has delivered your enemy into your hand. Kill him!"*

It would have been justified. It was self-defense. But David refuses. He says, *"The Lord forbid that I should do this thing to my lord, the Lord's anointed"* (1 Samuel 24:6).

Instead, David sneaks up and quietly cuts off a corner of Saul's robe.

When Saul leaves the cave, David follows him out. He bows down. He calls him "My lord the king!" He shows him the piece of fabric and says, essentially, *"Look. I could have killed you, but I didn't. I have no ill will toward you. I have forgiven you."*

Saul weeps. He acknowledges David is righteous. There is a moment of profound, emotional reconciliation.

But watch what happens next. This is the part we miss.

Saul says, *"Come back with me."*

And the text says: *"Then Saul went home, but David and his men went up to the stronghold"* (1 Samuel 24:22).

David didn't go back.

David forgave Saul. He honored Saul. He refused to harm Saul. He wished Saul well.

But he did not get in the chariot. He did not go back to the palace. He went back to the stronghold (the fortress).

Why? Because David knew something vital: **Saul was sorry, but Saul was not safe.**

David knew that Saul's tears were real, but his patterns were dangerous. David knew that forgiveness didn't mean he had to offer himself up as a target again.

He loved Saul from the cave. He honored Saul from the wilderness.

You can do the same.

You can forgive your father for his alcoholism, and still refuse to let him drive your children.

You can forgive your friend for her betrayal, and still decide she doesn't get to be in your inner circle anymore.

You can forgive your ex-spouse and still communicate only through a lawyer.

That is not a grudge. That is the "David Boundary." It says: *I will not harm you, but I will not let you harm me.*

Grace Without Proximity

This brings us to a concept I call "**Grace Without Proximity.**"

We often think that "grace" means "access." We think that if we are full of grace, we should have an open-door policy. But grace is unmerited favor. It is kindness. It is blessing. You can offer all of those things from a distance.

I worked with a woman named Elena whose sister was deeply manipulative. For years, Elena rode the roller coaster, rescuing her sister,

158

getting abused, forgiving her, letting her back in, and getting burned again. Finally, Elena set a hard boundary. She stopped the daily calls and the financial bailouts. She told me, weeping, "I feel like I've abandoned her."

We re-framed it. I asked her, *"How can you love her from here? How can you extend grace without extending proximity?"*

Elena realized she could pray for her sister, speak well of her, and send birthday cards, all while keeping her own door locked. That wasn't cruelty; it was a severe mercy.

CASE STUDY: THE "PRODIGAL SON'S BROTHER" (DEALING WITH FAMILY PRESSURE)

But what happens when the pressure to "forgive and forget" doesn't come from the toxic person, but from the rest of the family?

Let's talk about James. James has a younger brother, Chris, who struggles with addiction and narcissism. Every holiday, Chris causes a scene. He gets drunk, he insults James's wife, and he steals money.

James finally set a boundary: "I will not attend Christmas if Chris is there."

Chris didn't care. But James's mother, a sweet, conflict-avoidant woman, was devastated. She started calling James every day.

"James, it's Christmas. He's your brother. He cried to me on the phone yesterday; he's really sorry this time. Please, just be the bigger person. Don't tear the family apart."

James felt a crushing weight. He wasn't just fighting his brother's behavior; he was fighting his mother's disappointment.

This is a classic dynamic involving what family therapists call **Triangulation**. The mother is trying to stabilize the family by pressuring the healthiest person (James) to absorb the dysfunction of the unhealthiest person (Chris).

James had to set a boundary not just with Chris, but with his mother.

He had to say: *"Mom, I love you, and I love Chris. I have forgiven him. But forgiveness doesn't mean I expose my wife to abuse. I am not 'tearing the family apart'; I am protecting my family. I know you want everyone together, but I am staying home this year. And I need you to respect that decision if we are going to talk about this."*

Sometimes, practicing "Grace Without Proximity" means disappointing the "Peacemakers" in your life who just want everyone to get along at your expense. James realized that keeping the peace for his mom was costing him the peace of his own home. He chose his home.

The Forgiveness vs. Access Tool

When you are feeling confused, when the guilt makes you feel numb, and you can't tell if you are being wise or just mean, I want you to use this tool.

Draw a line down the middle of a piece of paper. On one side, write **Forgiveness**. On the other write, **Access**.

Let's look at the difference side-by-side.

- **First**, Forgiveness is a Command; we are instructed to do it. But Access is a Choice; we are wise to discern trust.
- **Second**, Forgiveness is Free; it costs them nothing. But Access is Earned; it costs them change.
- **Third**, Forgiveness takes One Person; you can do it alone. But Access takes Two People; it requires mutual safety.
- **Fourth**, Forgiveness is Past Tense; it deals with what happened. But Access is Future Tense; it deals with what *will* happen.
- **Finally**, Forgiveness is Unlimited; seventy times seven. But Access is Conditional; it is dependent on safety."

Look at that list. You can give the left column fully, 100%, while giving the right column 0%.

You can release the penalty (Forgiveness) while withholding the privilege (Access).

Jesus did this. There is a passage in John 2:23-24 that says, *"Many people saw the signs he was performing and believed in his name. But Jesus would not entrust himself to them, for he knew all people."*

Did you catch that? They believed in Him. But He did not **entrust** Himself to them.

Jesus forgave the world. He died for the world. But He only entrusted Himself to a few. He had boundaries around His heart. He knew that not everyone who wanted a piece of Him was safe for Him.

What About "The Work" of Restoration? (The Fruit Inspection)

Now, I want to be clear. Restoration is beautiful. Reconciliation is the heart of the Gospel. If the person who hurt you is willing to do the work, then yes, you can slowly begin to unlock the gate.

But how do you know if they are doing the work? How do you know if their apology is real?

We need to look at Matthew 7:16: *"By their fruit you will recognize them."*

Jesus didn't say, "By their tears you will recognize them." He didn't say, "By their eloquent apologies you will recognize them." He said **fruit**.

For the anxious attacher, this is tricky. We are so desperate for connection that we often mistake **Blossoms** for **Fruit**.

The Blossom (Fake Fruit)

- **What it looks like:** Crying, begging, grand gestures, flowers, long texts saying "I'm the worst, please forgive me," promises of "I'll never do it again."
- **The Trap:** Blossoms are beautiful, but they are fragile. A strong wind blows them away. Just because a tree has blossoms doesn't mean it will produce an apple. Many abusive people are experts at "Blossoming" to get you back.
- **Your Reaction:** You feel relief. You think, *Oh good, they get it! I can open the gate.*

The Harvest (Real Fruit)

- **What it looks like:** Changed behavior over a long period of time. Respecting your "No" without throwing a tantrum. Going to therapy and actually doing the work. Listening to your pain without making it about their guilt.
- **The Reality:** Fruit takes a season to grow. You cannot see fruit in a day. You cannot see fruit in a week.
- **Your Reaction:** You wait. You watch.

When someone apologizes, you are seeing a blossom. Do not eat the blossom. You have to wait for the harvest.

If you open the gate the moment they apologize, you are setting yourself up for the same cycle. True restoration requires a Waiting Season.

DEALING WITH THE "MEAN CHRISTIAN" LABEL

Even if you do this perfectly, even if you have the heart of David and the wisdom of Solomon, someone is going to call you mean.

Someone, likely the person you are setting boundaries with, is going to say:

"I thought you were a Christian. Christians are supposed to forgive. You're holding a grudge."

This is a weaponized theology. It is a manipulation tactic designed to use your own faith against you to get what they want.

When this happens, you need a script. You need words that acknowledge your forgiveness but hold your boundary.

The "Not Ready Yet" Scripts

- **The Timeline Script:** "I appreciate your apology, and I have forgiven you. However, forgiveness is instant, but trust is rebuilt slowly. I am not ready to go back to how things were yet. I need you to respect my pace."
- **The Safety Script:** "I love you, but I don't feel safe in this relationship right now. I'm taking a step back to heal. That doesn't mean I'm holding a grudge; it means I'm taking care of myself."
- **The "Fruit" Script:** "I hear that you want to change, and I hope you do. But I need to see that change in action over time before I can open this door again."

Do not let them play the God Card to override your wisdom.

CONCLUSION: THE FREEDOM OF THE CLEAN SLATE

The beauty of true forgiveness, the kind that doesn't require reconciliation, is that it sets you free.

When you think you have to reconcile with everyone you forgive, you will be hesitant to forgive. You will hold onto your anger as a shield because you think, *If I forgive them, I have to let them back in, and I can't do that.*

So you stay bitter to stay safe.

But once you realize that **Forgiveness ≠ Access**, you are free to forgive wildly!

You can forgive the abusive ex. You can forgive the toxic parent. You can forgive the friend who betrayed you. You can wash the slate clean of all debt, because you know you have a lock on the door.

You can say, "I release you completely," and in the same breath say, "And you are not allowed in my house." That is not a contradiction. That is the fullness of the Gospel. It is Grace (I release you) and Truth (I protect this).

You are not holding a grudge, friend. You are holding a boundary. And there is a world of difference.

Remember Maggie from Chapter 3? The one who wrote her brother David's resume? She finally handed him back his "knapsack." It was messy. David was angry for months. He actually lost his apartment and had to move in with a friend.

Maggie cried every day, feeling like she had failed him. But six months later, David got a job. A small one. One he found himself. Maggie didn't fix him, but by stepping out of the way, she finally allowed him to grow up. And for the first time in ten years, Maggie is sleeping through the night.

THE BOUNDARY BUILDER: THE FORGIVENESS AUDIT

Before we move on to what secure love actually looks like in the next chapter, I want you to do a spiritual audit. We are going to separate the debt from the gate.

Name the Person.

Who is the person you feel guilty about "not forgiving" because you are keeping a boundary?

The Grudge Check.

Ask yourself honestly: Do I wish them harm? Am I replaying their failure to make them look bad?

(If yes, pray: "Lord, I release my right to retaliate. I hand this justice to You.")

The Safety Check.

Why is the boundary there? Is it because they are currently unsafe (emotionally, physically, spiritually)?

(If yes, affirm: "My boundary is a wise wall, not a weapon.")

The "Grace from Afar" Action.

What is one way you can wish them well without opening the gate?

(Example: Pray for them for 30 seconds. Release a specific debt they owe you. Bless them in your heart.)

The Gatekeeper's Truth:

Write this sentence in your journal:

"I can forgive [Name] fully and still choose not to trust them. My forgiveness is their gift; my trust is my stewardship."

You are clean. You are safe. Let's keep going.

12

LOVING WITHOUT
LOSING YOURSELF

I remember the first time I realized my marriage had changed.

It wasn't during a romantic candlelight dinner. It wasn't during a grand apology or a massive breakthrough conversation. It was on a Tuesday evening. My husband and I were sitting on the couch. He was reading a book. I was folding laundry. The TV was off. The house was quiet.

And for the first time in my life, my internal alarm system was silent.

For years, a quiet Tuesday would have filled me with a heavy, silent dread. *Is he mad? Why isn't he talking to me? Is the distance between us on this couch a sign of emotional distance? Do I need to ask him a question to check the temperature? Should I fix something?*

In the past, my body would have gone numb. I would have felt that familiar slump in my stomach, the fawn response kicking in, urging me to make myself smaller, sweeter, or more helpful just to ensure I was safe.

But that night, I checked my body. My stomach was soft. My chest was open. There was no heaviness in my limbs. I looked at him, and I didn't feel the frantic need to do anything to earn his love.

I realized, with a jolt of surprise: *Oh. This is what safety feels like.*

It felt... boring.

And it was the most beautiful boredom I had ever experienced.

If you have spent your life in the cycle of anxious attachment, people-pleasing, and over-functioning, you are likely addicted to adrenaline. You are used to love feeling like a roller coaster: the high of being needed, the low of being rejected, the loop-de-loop of fixing a crisis. You mistake intensity for intimacy.

So, when you finally do the work, when you set the boundaries, weather the pushback, and establish a new rhythm, you might find yourself feeling unsettled. You might look at your life and think, *Is this it? Is this all there is?*

Because there is no drama to fix, you feel useless. Because there is no crisis to manage, you feel invisible.

In this chapter, we are going to talk about the hardest part of recovery: Learning to tolerate peace.

We are going to explore what it looks like to love someone without losing yourself in the process. We are going to redefine "excitement." And we are going to learn how to enjoy the garden you have fought so hard to fence in.

The Withdrawal from Chaos

When you stop over-functioning, the first thing you will notice is the space.

You used to spend 80% of your mental energy managing other people's emotions. *Is Mom okay? Is my boss mad? Did I upset my friend?* Now that you have given those responsibilities back to their owners (remember the "Yards" from Chapter 7?), you have a massive surplus of energy.

And if you aren't careful, you will try to fill it with new anxiety. You will invent problems because your brain is trying to reach its baseline level of stress. But we are going to resist that urge. We are going to learn to sit in the quiet without assuming it means danger.

THE "NEW NORMAL" OF RECIPROCITY (THE SEE-SAW EFFECT)

For years, your relationships have operated like a broken see-saw. You were the one on the ground, pushing up with all your might, using your legs, your back, your spirit, to keep the other person lifted high. You did the planning. You did the emotional regulating. You did the apologizing. You did the initiating.

You were exhausted, but you were in control. As long as you were doing the work, you knew the see-saw wouldn't crash. You knew exactly where you stood.

But when you set boundaries, you stopped pushing. You stood up. You took your seat on the other side of the see-saw, and you waited.

This is the scariest moment in the transition to secure love. It is the moment of Reciprocity.

When you stop over-functioning, you create a vacuum. You create a space where the other person has to act if the relationship is going to work. And for a while, there might be silence. There might be a wobble.

I worked with a woman named Julie who was the "Social Cruise Director" of her friend group. She planned every birthday, every baby shower, and every coffee date. If she didn't text first, they didn't talk. When she finally decided to set a boundary and stop initiating every single interaction, she was terrified.

She told me, "If I don't text them, we won't talk for a month."

I told her, "Then you need to know that. You need to know if you have a friendship or a ministry."

So she stopped. And for three weeks, her phone was quiet. The silence was agonizing. She felt the heavy dread of rejection settling in her chest. She felt like she was disappearing. This is the "void" that boundaries create. It exposes the reality of the relationship.

But then, in week four, a text came through. "Hey! I haven't heard from you in a while. I miss your face. Want to get dinner?"

Julie wept. Not because she got a dinner date, but because of what that text represented. For the first time in ten years, she wasn't making the friendship happen. She was *receiving* friendship.

This is the shift. Secure love requires two active participants. It requires Reciprocity.

Reciprocity isn't a strict 50/50 split every single day; sometimes you carry 80% because they are sick, and sometimes they carry 80% because you are grieving. But over the arc of the relationship, there is a mutual exchange of care, effort, and initiation.

When you hold your ground and let the silence sit, the other person finally has the room to realize you aren't doing it for them anymore. They realize the "automatic door" of your effort has stopped opening, and they have to reach out and turn the handle themselves.

Your husband, realizing you haven't planned the date night, asks, "Hey, do you want to grab tacos on Friday?" Your mom, realizing you aren't going to fix the family drama, calls just to talk about the weather.

When this happens, you will feel a strange sensation. It is the feeling of being loved not for what you do, but for who you are. You didn't earn that text. You didn't buy that date night with your labor. You received it.

This is the shift from "Earning" to "Receiving." Secure love is not a wage you work for; it is a gift you allow in.

The Shock of Safety (Why "Boring" Feels Wrong)

We need to talk about the "B" word. *Boring.*

In our culture, and especially in romantic comedies, love is depicted as a high-stakes drama. It's chasing someone through an airport. It's screaming matches in the rain followed by passionate make-ups. It's the constant wondering: *Do they love me? Do they not?*

To a nervous system that has been wired for anxiety, consistency feels incredibly boring. In fact, it can feel suspicious. It can even feel like apathy.

When you are used to the "high" of saving the day, or the "low" of fearing abandonment, a steady Tuesday evening where everyone is just... fine... feels like something is wrong.

I call this the Adrenaline Withdrawal.

If you have spent decades eating the "fast food" of toxic relationships, high sugar, high salt, instant gratification, instant crash, a healthy, home-cooked meal of secure love is going to taste bland at first. You are going to miss the spike. You are going to miss the rush of fixing a crisis and feeling like a hero.

You might find yourself picking a fight just to feel something. You might find yourself inventing a problem just to solve it. You might look at your calm, steady spouse and think, *Maybe I'm just not in love anymore because I don't feel that butterflies-in-the-stomach anxiety.*

But your nervous system isn't firing because you aren't scanning for a threat. You aren't holding your breath waiting for the other shoe to drop.

When this happens, I want you to whisper a new truth to yourself: "Peace is not the absence of love. Peace is the presence of safety."

Secure love is often quiet. It is rhythmic. It is the steady heartbeat, not the skipping one.

It is knowing your partner will come home when they say they will. It is knowing your friend isn't mad at you just because she hasn't texted back in two hours. It is knowing that you can make a mistake and you won't be exiled.

This "boredom" is actually the fertile soil where your real life can finally grow. When you aren't spending all your energy managing the relationship, you have energy to write the book. To start the business. To play with your kids. To deepen your walk with God.

Drama consumes your life. Safety expands it.

THE "NO" THAT BUILDS INTIMACY (VOLUNTARY LOVE)

The hallmark of secure love, the thing that separates it from codependency, is the safety of the "No."

In an anxious relationship, "No" is a dirty word. "No" is a rejection. "No" is a threat. If you say "No," the relationship might crumble. If they say "No," you feel unloved.

In a secure relationship, "No" is just information.

But more than that, the "No" is what makes the "Yes" real. I want you to picture a house. If you invite someone over, but you lock the doors from the outside so they can never leave, are they a guest? No. They are a hostage.

A hostage might tell you they love you. They might eat dinner with you. They might smile at you. But you will never truly know if they want to be there, because they have no choice.

Boundaries unlock the door.

When you allow someone to say "No" to you, to your request, your invite, your preference, you are unlocking the door. You are giving them the freedom to leave. And if they stay? If they say "Yes" next time? You know it is real.

171

I remember the first time I set a small boundary with a secure friend. She asked me to help with a project, and I was swamped. My old instinct was to say, "Yes, of course!" and then stay up until 2:00 AM resenting her, driven by that heavy dread of disappointing her.

Instead, I used the scripts we learned. I said, "I love you, and I love this project, but I'm at capacity this week, so I can't help."

I braced for impact. I waited for the cold shoulder. I waited for the guilt trip.

She texted back: "Totally get it! Proud of you for protecting your time. Let's grab coffee when you're free."

I stared at the phone. That's it? She wasn't mad? She still wanted coffee?

I realized then that my "Yes" had been a lie for years. I had been giving a "Yes" born of fear, not of love. But now, because she accepted my "No," my next "Yes" to her was 100% real. It was Voluntary Love.

Secure love allows for separate needs. It allows for the reality that we are two different people with two different capacity levels.

You can say "No" to sex tonight, and your husband doesn't pout or question your attraction to him; he just kisses your forehead and says, "Okay, let's get some sleep." You can say "No" to the church committee, and the pastor doesn't question your faith; he thanks you for your honesty.

When you realize that the relationship can survive your boundaries, a heavy weight lifts off your shoulders. You realize you are not a hostage, and neither are they. You are volunteers. And volunteers serve with a lot more joy than prisoners do.

The Art of Receiving (Putting Down the Ledger)

There is one more hurdle to clear in this "Integration" phase, and it might be the hardest one of all. You have to learn how to receive.

For the anxious attacher or the chronic helper, giving is easy. Giving is power. When you are the one giving the help, the money, the advice, or the time, you are in the safe position. You are the creditor. They owe you.

Receiving, however, is vulnerable. Receiving means you have a need. Receiving means you are in debt (or so your brain tells you).

When someone does something nice for you, when they pay for lunch, or offer to watch your kids, or give you a compliment, do you immediately scramble to pay them back? Do you deflect the compliment? (*"Oh this old shirt? It was on sale."*) Do you immediately say, *"I'll get the next one!"*?

This is the "Transactional Ledger" at work. You are terrified of owing anyone anything because, in the past, people used your debt to manipulate you.

But in secure love, we burn the ledger.

Loving without losing yourself means allowing yourself to be poured into. It means acknowledging that you are human, you are finite, and you have needs.

The next time someone offers you kindness, I want you to practice the "Full Stop."

Them: "You look beautiful today." **You:** "Thank you." (Full stop. Do not explain the outfit. Do not compliment them back immediately.)

Them: "Let me pick up the check." **You:** "That is so kind of you. Thank you." (Full stop. Do not promise to buy them a house next week.)

Allowing someone to love you is a gift to them. It allows them the joy of giving. When you deflect every kindness, you are robbing them of that joy. You are keeping the gate locked tight.

Open the gate. Let the love come in. You don't have to pay for it.

Your Taste Buds Change (Choosing Safe People)

Here is the most surprising fruit of this journey: You will stop being attracted to people who need saving.

For a long time, your "type", whether in friends or partners, was probably "The Project." You were drawn to the person with the sad eyes, the chaotic life, the "potential." You loved them because they needed you. You felt valuable because you were the only one who could understand them, fix them, or tolerate them.

But as you heal, as you install your gates and tend your garden, your taste buds change.

You start to lose your appetite for chaos. You start to find "The Project" exhausting rather than endearing. You start to crave people who are already whole.

You begin to look for partners and friends who bring their own "backpack" (remember Chapter 3?) rather than asking you to carry it. You begin to value consistency over intensity. You begin to value kindness over charisma.

This can be disorienting. You might look at a new friend who is steady, reliable, and undramatic, and think, *We don't have chemistry.* But often, what we call "chemistry" is just anxiety. It's the spark of dysfunction recognizing dysfunction.

True connection is the calm recognition of safety. It is the feeling of Shalom.

You will find yourself drawn to people who:

- Respect your "No" the first time.
- Apologize when they are wrong without making excuses.
- Ask about your life and actually listen to the answer.
- Have their own hobbies, friends, and relationship with God.

You are upgrading your community. You are building a circle of "Safe People."

PRACTICAL APPLICATION: THE GREEN FLAGS CHECKLIST

We talk a lot about Red Flags, the warning signs of toxic behavior. But when you are learning a new language of love, you need to know what to look for, not just what to look *out* for.

Here is a checklist of Secure Love Indicators. These are the five specific Green Flags that tell you a relationship is a safe place to plant your garden.

Green Flag Number One is The "No" Test. You know this is present when you say "no" or set a limit, and they accept it without punishing you, guilt-tripping you, or giving you the silent treatment. This matters because it shows they value your personhood more than your compliance.

Green Flag Number Two is The Repair Cycle. In a safe relationship, when you have a conflict, you can actually talk about it. They take ownership of their part, saying things like, "I'm sorry I raised my voice", without blaming you or claiming, "I only yelled because you made me mad." This is vital because conflict is inevitable, but repair is optional. Safe people prioritize the repair.

Green Flag Number Three is The Reciprocity Check. Look for a dynamic where they initiate contact, plans, and care roughly as often as you do. You do not feel like you are "carrying" the relationship. This balance proves that the relationship is voluntary, rather than being sustained solely by your over-functioning.

Green Flag Number Four is The "Separate Self" Respect. A safe partner or friend encourages your hobbies, your other friendships, and your alone time. They celebrate your wins without jealousy. Remember: Enmeshment is not intimacy. A safe person wants you to be *more* of yourself, not less.

Finally, Green Flag Number Five is The Consistency Factor. This means their actions match their words. They are the same person in public as they are in private, and you don't have to guess what "mood version" of them you are going to get today. This matters because consistency calms the nervous system. It creates the "trust bank account" we talked about in Chapter 11.

If you look at your life and see these Green Flags, pause and give thanks. This is the fruit of your labor. This is what you have been fighting for.

A NOTE TO THE SINGLE WOMAN (OR THE LONELY WIFE)

I know some of you are reading this checklist and feeling a pang of grief. Maybe you look at your marriage, and you don't see these flags. Maybe you are single, and you feel like these men don't exist.

I want to speak tenderly to you. Recognizing what is absent is the first step toward change.

If you are in a marriage that lacks these things, you are doing the good work of becoming the "Safe Person" first. You are changing the dance. You are bringing the Green Flags into the room. As we discussed in Chapter 10, when one person changes, the system must change. Keep holding the line. Keep offering the invitation to health.

If you are single, let this list be your new standard. Do not settle for the "fixer-upper" because you are lonely. Your solitude is safer than a toxic relationship. Wait for the Green Flags. Wait for the person who has their own gate.

Living in the Exhale

Ultimately, loving without losing yourself feels like a long, deep exhale.

It is the feeling of taking off tight shoes at the end of a long day. You can wiggle your toes. You can breathe. You are home.

For so long, you believed the lie that you had to shrink to fit into someone else's life. You believed you had to chop off parts of your personality, your needs, and your voice to be digestible.

But secure love expands to make room for you. It delights in your wholeness. It wants the real you, the you with limits, the you with opinions, the you with needs, because that is the only version of you that is actually alive.

God did not design you to be a doormat. He designed you to be a temple. A temple has walls. It has gates. But inside? Inside, it is filled with glory.

You have done the demolition work. You have built the walls. You have hung the gate. Now, my friend, it is time to enjoy the glory.

THE BOUNDARY BUILDER: SAVORING SAFETY

We are so good at scanning for danger that we often forget to scan for safety. We need to retrain your brain to register peace as "good" rather than "boring."

I want you to take five minutes today to do a Safety Scan.

1. **Find a moment of Reciprocity.** Did someone open a door for you? Did a friend text you back? Did your spouse make the

coffee?

- ○ **Action:** Stop. Name it. Say to yourself, *"I am receiving care. I didn't earn this. It is a gift."*

2. **Find a moment of Permission.** Did you feel tired and decide to sit down? Did you leave the dishes in the sink to go read a book?
   - ○ **Action:** Stop. Name it. Say to yourself, *"I am listening to my body. I am allowed to rest. The world is not ending."*
3. **Find a moment of Connection.** Look at a "Safe Person" in your life (or even a pet!). Look at their eyes.
   - ○ **Action:** Take a deep breath. Say to yourself, *"I am safe with this person. I don't have to perform. I can just be."*

Let your nervous system soak in that truth like a dry sponge in water. You are safe. You are whole. You are loved.

The Gatekeeper's Truth

> *"The boundary lines have fallen for me in pleasant places; surely I have a delightful inheritance."*

— PSALM 16:6

Reflection: Safety might feel boring at first, but it is the only place where you can truly inherit the life God has for you. The boundaries you have set are not walls of isolation; they are the lines that define your pleasant place. Enjoy your inheritance.

13

WHEN TO ADJUST
AND WHEN TO HOLD

There is a specific danger that happens about six months to a year after you start living with healthy boundaries.

You have survived the initial guilt. You have weathered the pushback. You have built your fence, installed your gate, and started to enjoy the peace in your own backyard. You feel strong. You feel protected. The silence, which used to feel heavy and oppressive, has become a friend.

But then, something shifts.

Maybe the friend who used to drain you actually goes to therapy, apologizes, and starts taking responsibility for her own life. Maybe your mother, who used to guilt-trip you every Sunday, finally accepts your "once a month" rule and starts being pleasant again. Maybe *you* change. You walk out of a season of deep burnout, you get some sleep, you heal, and you feel your capacity returning.

And you find yourself standing at the gate you built, looking at the lock you installed, and wondering: *Is it okay to open this?*

This is the moment where the "Recovering Doormat" often freezes. We are so conditioned to the days of being trampled that we tend to over-correct. We confuse Strength with Rigidity. We swing the pendulum from "I have no walls" to "I live in a bunker."

We think, *If I move this line, I'm caving. If I answer that text, I'm sliding back. If I say yes today after saying no yesterday, I'm a hypocrite.*

So, we keep the walls up, high and thick, even when the storm has passed. We become like a person who boards up their windows for a hurricane, nailing the plywood shut with a heavy, robotic determination. But then, the storm passes. The sun comes out. It is a beautiful July day. But we leave the plywood up "just in case." Inside the house, it is dark, stuffy, and airless. We are safe, yes. But we are not living.

That isn't safety. That is a prison.

In this chapter, we are going to learn the advanced skill of **Boundary Stewardship**. We are going to learn that boundaries are not dead stones that we set once and leave forever. They are living things. They are fences with gates that are designed to swing.

True wisdom is not about holding the line at all costs. True wisdom is knowing when to hold, when to fold, and when to expand. It is about trusting yourself enough to know that you can open the door without taking it off the hinges.

The Difference Between "Caving" and "Adjusting"

The dread you feel when you think about relaxing a boundary is valid. You remember the pain of the "Porous Life" (Chapter 7), and you never want to go back there. You remember the exhaustion of the "Resentful Yes."

But there is a massive difference between **Caving** and **Adjusting**. They look the same on the outside; in both cases, the line moves, but the internal mechanics are completely different.

Caving happens when you move a boundary because of External Pressure.

- **The Driver:** Fear and Fawning.
- **The Thought:** "They are mad at me, so I better change." "If I don't do this, I'll lose the relationship." "I just need to fix this so the tension stops."
- **The Result:** You feel resentful, numb, and defeated. You have surrendered your territory to keep the peace.

Adjusting happens when you move a boundary because of Internal Wisdom.

- **The Driver:** Love and Safety.
- **The Thought:** "The situation has healed, or my capacity has increased, so I choose to open the gate." "I want to let them in because I trust myself to handle it."
- **The Result:** You feel generous, empowered, and free. You have expanded your territory to include connection.

You are the Gatekeeper. And a good Gatekeeper doesn't just lock the door and swallow the key. A good Gatekeeper watches the horizon, checks the weather, and decides, day by day, what belongs inside and what belongs outside.

SEASONAL BOUNDARIES: THE ECCLESIASTES PRINCIPLE

One of the biggest lies we believe about boundaries is that they are statutes carved in stone. We think, *I have told my mother-in-law she cannot drop by unannounced. That is the rule forever. Amen.*

But life is not static. Life is seasonal.

God created the seasons. He created Winter, where resources are scarce, the ground is hard, and the primary goal is survival. And He created Summer, where resources are abundant, the sun is high, and the goal is growth and connection.

Your boundaries should reflect the season of your soul. A coat that saves your life in January will give you heatstroke in July. If you wear your "Winter Boundaries" into your "Summer Season," you will suffer unnecessary isolation.

The Winter Season (Survival Mode) There are times in your life when your capacity is naturally low. Perhaps you are in a "Winter" season:

- You just had a baby (postpartum is a severe, biological winter).
- You are grieving a loss.
- You are recovering from a health crisis or burnout.
- You are in a high-stress season at work or supporting a crisis in your immediate family.

In a Winter season, you need **Rigid Boundaries**. You cannot afford to have the gate open. You need to conserve heat. You need to say "No" to almost everything that isn't essential survival.

During a Winter season, you might say to a needy friend: *"I love you, but I cannot process heavy emotional stuff right now. I need to take a break from our weekly calls until I get my feet back under me."*

That is not cruel. That is hibernation. It is necessary for life. If you try to keep the gate open during a blizzard, the pipes burst.

The Summer Season (Growth Mode), but Winter doesn't last forever. Eventually, the fog lifts. The baby sleeps through the night. The grief softens. Your energy returns. The crisis stabilizes.

In a Summer season, you have a surplus. Your "shed" (from Chapter 7) is stocked. When you are in Summer, keeping the heavy, rigid boundaries of Winter doesn't protect you anymore; it isolates you. It keeps you from the joy of community.

In Summer, you might say to that same friend: *"Hey, I'm feeling much stronger. I'd love to grab coffee and hear what's been going on with you."*

This is the key: **A boundary that saved you in Winter might suffocate you in Summer.**

I see so many women feel guilty about this shift. They think, *If I let her back in now, wasn't I lying when I said I needed space six months ago? Am I being inconsistent?*

No. You were telling the truth for that season. You are allowed to thaw. You are allowed to expand. Your boundaries are allowed to breathe as you breathe. Consistency is not "doing the same thing forever." Consistency is "staying true to reality." When reality changes, the boundary must change to match it.

CASE STUDY: THE SHIFT

To understand what this looks like in the messy reality of life, let's talk about Lisa.

Lisa grew up with a mother who was the definition of "unsafe." Her mother was critical, intrusive, and emotionally volatile. She would call Lisa ten times a day, demand money, and verbally abuse Lisa if she didn't comply. For years, Lisa was the Doormat.

Then, Lisa found her voice. She went to therapy, read the books, and set a hard, "Winter" boundary. She told her mother: *"I will speak to you once a week on Sunday. If you yell, I will hang up. I will not give you money."*

For two years, Lisa held this line. It was hard, but it gave her peace. Her marriage improved. Her anxiety dropped. She felt safe behind her wall.

Then, the phone rang on a Tuesday. It was the hospital. Her mother had suffered a massive stroke.

Suddenly, the landscape changed. The mother, who was a terrifying, dominating force, was now lying in a hospital bed, unable to speak, unable to move the left side of her body. The power dynamic had flipped overnight.

Lisa stood at a crossroads that filled her with dread. The "Rigid" voice in her head warned: *Don't go! It's a trap! You promised yourself you wouldn't get sucked back in. If you go to the hospital, you're breaking your own rules. You're failing.* But the "Spirit" voice in her head whispered: *The season has changed. The threat level has dropped. You are strong enough to offer mercy now.*

Lisa called me, her voice tight with anxiety. "Am I crazy for wanting to go care for her? Does this mean I have no boundaries?"

We looked at the situation through the lens of Adjusting, not Caving. Was Lisa going because she was afraid of her mother? No. Her mother couldn't even speak. Was Lisa going because she felt obligated? A little, yes. But mostly, Lisa was going because she was a daughter who wanted to honor her mother in a time of crisis, and she assessed that she had the strength to do it without losing herself.

Lisa decided to shift from a Rigid Boundary to a Flexible Boundary. She went to the hospital. She became her mother's advocate with the doctors. She sat by the bed and held her hand.

But, and this is vital, she did not become Porous. When the discharge planner asked if her mother could move in with Lisa, Lisa felt the old heaviness rising in her chest. The old Lisa would have said "Yes" out of a fawn response, just to avoid the conflict. The old Lisa would have destroyed her own home to save her mother. But the new, flexible Lisa said: *"No. That is not possible. We need to find a skilled nursing facility."*

She opened the gate enough to let mercy out, but she kept the chain on the door so chaos couldn't get in. She adjusted for the season (illness) without abandoning her core need for safety. That is the art of the shift.

FLEXIBLE VS. POROUS: THE INTENTIONAL GATE

So, how do we know if we are being "Flexible" (healthy) or "Porous" (unhealthy)? They can look similar on the outside, both involve saying "Yes" where we once said "No", but the internal mechanics are completely different.

Think of the plumbing in your house.

First, let's look at **Porous Boundaries**, a leaky faucet. Water is dripping out, not because you turned the handle, but because the washer is broken. You are losing water against your will. You feel helpless, frustrated, and drained. You try to stop it, but you can't. The resource (water/energy) is being stolen from you drop by drop.

Porous Boundaries are a leaky faucet. Water is dripping out, not because you turned the handle, but because the washer is broken. You are losing water against your will. You feel helpless, frustrated, and drained. You try to stop it, but you can't. The resource, your energy, is being stolen from you drop by drop.

Flexible Boundaries are a kitchen tap. You walk over, turn the handle, and let the water flow because you want to fill a pitcher. You have a purpose. Then, when the pitcher is full, you turn it off. You are in control of the flow. You are not losing water; you are dispensing it.

Let's look at the difference side-by-side to help you discern where you are standing.

First, let's look at the Porous Boundary, or "**The Leak.**" This style is driven by fear, guilt, or external pressure. The internal thought process usually sounds like, "If I don't do this, they will leave me," or "I have to fix this to keep the peace." The result is that you feel resentful, numb, and defeated. You feel this way because you have surrendered your agency.

Now, compare that to the Flexible Boundary, or "**The Tap.**" This style is driven by your values and a genuine choice to love. The internal thought process here sounds like, "I have the capacity to help right now, and I want to," or "I am choosing to extend grace in this moment." The result is that you feel generous and connected. You feel this way because you retained your agency.

If you are opening the gate because someone is banging on it and you want the noise to stop, that is Porous. If you are opening the gate because you looked through the peephole, saw a need, checked your own supplies, and decided to offer help, that is Flexible.

THE TROJAN HORSE WARNING: WHEN NOT TO OPEN

Now, we need to have a serious talk about safety. Because while seasons change, some people do not. There is a specific danger when we start to relax boundaries: **The Trojan Horse.**

In Greek mythology, the Greeks couldn't breach the walls of Troy. The walls were too strong. So they built a giant wooden horse, left it as a "gift," and sailed away. The Trojans, thinking they had won and the war was over, dragged the horse inside their gates. But inside the hollow belly of the horse were Greek soldiers. Once inside the walls, under the cover of night, they jumped out and destroyed the city.

Toxic people are excellent at building Trojan Horses. They know they can't force their way back into your life anymore; your walls are too high. You've stopped answering the guilt-trip texts. You've stopped lending money. So, they change tactics. They present something that looks like a gift to get you to open the gate yourself.

The Trojan Horse usually looks like:

- **The Sudden Spiritual Epiphany:** "God spoke to me last night. I realized I've been awful. I'm a totally new person." (But it's only been three days).
- **The Over-the-Top Gift:** Sending money, lavish presents, or grand gestures of affection after a period of silence.

- The "**Emergency**": Manufacturing a crisis to force you to break your "No Contact" rule.
- **The Charm Offensive:** Suddenly acting sickly sweet, complimenting you, and agreeing with everything you say. This is often called "Love Bombing."

How do you know if it's a Trojan Horse or a genuine olive branch? **You check for soldiers.**

You look for the hidden agenda. Genuine change is slow, humble, and consistent. Manipulative change is fast, loud, and urgent.

If you hesitate to open the gate for a genuinely changed person, they will say: *"I understand. I broke your trust, and it will take time to earn it back. Take all the time you need. I'm just here when you're ready."*

A Trojan Horse will say: *"After all I've done? You're still punishing me? I told you I changed! You're being so un-Christian!"*

The moment they meet resistance, the soldiers jump out of the horse. The anger returns. The guilt-tripping returns. And you see the truth: They didn't want connection; they wanted access.

If you see the soldiers, slam the gate. You are not being unforgiving. You are defending the city.

THE "SMALL OPENINGS" STRATEGY

So, let's say it's not a Trojan Horse. Let's say you genuinely think the person has grown, or you feel ready to try again. Maybe your spouse has been in therapy for six months, and things are calm. Maybe your friend has apologized and backed off. How do you open the gate without risking everything?

You use **Small Openings**.

You don't go from "Blocked Number" to "Week-long Family Vacation" in one jump. You test the bridge before you drive the eighteen-wheeler over it. We use the concept of Graduated Exposure.

Level 1: The Digital Test (Low Risk) Unblock the number. Respond to a text. Keep it brief and light.

- **The Test:** How does it feel? Did your stomach drop? Did they bombard you with 50 messages the second you replied? Did they immediately ask for a favor?
- **The Move:** If they flood you, you close the digital gate again. If they send a respectful, normal reply, you wait.

Level 2: The Public Neutral Ground (Medium Risk) A brief, public meeting. Coffee for 45 minutes. Not dinner. Not your house.

- **The Logistics:** You drive your own car (so you can leave). You have a hard "out" time ("I have to leave at 11:00").
- **The Test:** Do they respect the end time? Do they try to guilt you into staying? Do they start the old drama?
- **The Move:** If they respect the limit, you mark it as a "Win." If they cause a scene, you leave, and you return to Level 1.

Level 3: The Inner Circle (Higher Risk) A dinner at your home. A longer conversation. Vulnerability.

- **The Test:** Can they handle your real heart? Can they handle Reciprocity?
- **The Move:** This level is reserved for people who have passed Level 1 and Level 2 consistently over time.

This is the beauty of the Gate. It swings both ways. You can open it an inch, realize it's not safe, and close it again. You are not failing by closing it again; you are gathering data. You are acting as the Manager of the relationship.

DISCERNMENT: TRAUMA BRAIN VS. HOLY SPIRIT

One of the hardest parts of adjusting boundaries is knowing which voice to listen to. When you think about opening the gate, you will hear a voice saying "Danger!" But is that the voice of wisdom (The Holy Spirit) warning you of a real threat? Or is that the voice of trauma (The Amygdala) remembering an old pain that is no longer there?

We need to learn to distinguish the two.

Trauma Brain speaks in absolutes and urgency.

- **It sounds like:** "NEVER! ALWAYS! YOU HAVE TO FIX THIS! SUBMIT!"
- **It feels like:** Brain fog, sudden exhaustion, a slump in your shoulders, a numbness in your hands, or a frantic "I'm going to die if I don't make them happy."
- **Its goal:** Survival at all costs. It doesn't care about growth; it cares about not getting eaten.

The Holy Spirit (Wisdom) speaks in clarity and stillness.

- **It sounds like:** "Not yet." "Proceed with caution." "Check the fruit." "This is safe now."
- **It feels like:** A heavy "check" in your gut (if it's a no) or a grounded peace (if it's a yes). It is rarely frantic or numb.
- **Its goal:** Shalom (Wholeness). It cares about truth and health.

If you feel that sudden numbness or the urge to collapse and fawn, take a timeout. Regulate your body. Breathe. That is likely trauma. If you are feeling a steady, heavy resolve that says, "I just don't have peace about this," listen to it. That is likely the Spirit.

Don't let trauma make your decisions, but don't ignore the Spirit's warnings. The Spirit will never ask you to put yourself in a position where you are being abused. He may ask you to risk loving, but He will never ask you to partner with evil.

PRACTICAL ELEMENT: THE BOUNDARY REVIEW GUIDE

Discernment is a muscle. It gets stronger the more you use it. But in the beginning, it helps to have a checklist. Before you decide to relax a boundary, whether it's stepping down from a "No," letting someone back in, or taking on a new responsibility, I want you to run it through this diagnostic test.

The "Should I Adjust?" Checklist

1. The Internal Check (My Yard)

- **Am I moving this boundary out of fear or freedom?**
  - *Fear:* "I'm afraid they will hate me/leave me/gossip about me if I don't." (STOP. KEEP THE BOUNDARY.)
  - *Freedom:* "I feel rested, safe, and I genuinely want to engage." (PROCEED.)
- **Do I have the surplus resources?**
  - *Deficit:* "I am already exhausted, but I feel I should." (STOP. KEEP THE BOUNDARY.)
  - *Surplus:* "I have the time/money/energy to give this without resentment." (PROCEED.)

2. The External Check (Their Yard)

- **Has there been consistent, changed behavior over time?**
  - *No:* They are still doing the same things, but I just miss them/feel guilty. (STOP.)
  - *Yes:* They have respected my "No" and shown humility for at least 3–6 months. (PROCEED.)
- **Are they respecting the current boundary?**

- *No:* They are currently pushing against the fence or complaining about it. (STOP. TIGHTEN THE BOUNDARY.)
- *Yes:* They have accepted the limit gracefully. (SAFE TO OPEN A LITTLE.)

3. The Trojan Horse Scan

- **Is there urgency?**
  - *Yes:* "We need to fix this NOW." (WARNING: DO NOT OPEN.)
  - *No:* They are patient with my timeline. (SAFE.)

Write these questions down. Pray over them. Discuss them with a safe friend or your spouse. If you get "Green Lights" across the board, proceed with a Small Opening.

THE BOUNDARY BUILDER

I want to close this chapter by telling you something that might be hard to believe: *You are wise.*

If you are reading this book, you have spent a lifetime ignoring your own intuition. You have outsourced your wisdom to other people, to your parents, your pastor, your friends, your spouse. You have treated yourself like an unruly child who cannot be trusted to know what is safe. You have believed that everyone else knows better than you do.

But the Holy Spirit lives in you. Scripture says, *"But the Advocate, the Holy Spirit, whom the Father will send in my name, will teach you all things"* (John 14:26).

You have an internal teacher. You have a "check" in your spirit.

The Boundary Builder: Stand at the gate. Does your spirit feel heavy (Winter) or light (Summer)? Trust the season you are in, not the season you wish you were in.

You are the only one who knows the state of your garden. You are the only one who knows if it is Winter or Summer in your soul. God has entrusted the keys to you. Stop asking everyone else if you are allowed to unlock the door. You are the owner. Trust what you know.

The Gatekeeper's Truth

"There is a time for everything, and a season for every activity under the heavens."

— ECCLESIASTES 3:1

Reflection: God does not demand a harvest in winter. Trust His timing for your open gates.

14

YOUR ONGOING RESET

There is a specific heaviness that sets in when you reach the last few pages of a self-help book.

You feel it right now, don't you?

For the last thirteen chapters, we have been walking together. We have dismantled the lies of people-pleasing, learned the scripts of healthy boundaries, and practiced the art of the "Holy Pause." You have felt understood. You have felt empowered. You have probably highlighted half this book and thought, *Yes! This is the new me!*

But now, you can feel the end approaching. And a quiet, heavy dread is starting to rise:

What happens on Monday morning?

What happens when I close this book and walk back into my real life, where my mother still knows exactly which buttons to push? What happens when I get tired, or sick, or overwhelmed, and I accidentally say "Yes" to a committee I hate?

Does that mean I failed? Do I have to start all over?

I want to pause right here and take that heavy backpack off your shoulders one last time.

The goal of this book was never to turn you into a Boundary Robot, a woman who never falters, never feels guilt, and never struggles to speak up. That woman doesn't exist. And frankly, she sounds exhausting.

The goal was to give you a Reset.

A reset is not a one-time event that fixes you forever. It is a tool you carry in your pocket. It is the ability to notice when you have drifted into fear and gently, kindly steer yourself back toward love.

You are going to mess this up. You are going to backslide. You are going to have weeks where you fall into the "Resentful Yes" and weeks where you act like a "Rigid Fortress."

And that is okay.

In this final chapter, we are not going to talk about how to be perfect. We are going to talk about how to be human. We are going to talk about how to live this out, imperfectly and beautifully, for the rest of your life.

THE MYTH OF THE WAGON

We often talk about growth like it's a wagon. We are either "on the wagon" (doing everything right, setting boundaries, drinking water, reading our Bible) or we are "off the wagon" (face down in the mud, saying yes to everyone, miserable).

This binary thinking is the enemy of secure love.

When you believe in the Wagon, a single mistake becomes a catastrophe. If you say "yes" to a favor you didn't want to do, you think, *Well, I blew it. I'm just a people-pleaser. I'll never change.* And you give up.

But boundaries are not a wagon you fall off of. They are a garden you tend.

TENDING VS. BUILDING

Think about the difference between building a fence and tending a garden.

Building a fence is hard, sweaty, heavy work. You have to dig post holes in rocky soil. You have to mix concrete. You have to carry heavy lumber. It is exhausting, and it requires a massive upfront investment of energy.

For the last thirteen chapters, we have been building. You have been digging up the rotten posts of codependency. You have been hauling the heavy lumber of truth. You have been installing the Gate we talked about in Chapter 7.

If you feel tired, that is why. You have been doing construction work on your soul.

But here is the good news: You don't have to build the fence every day.

Once the fence is built, the work changes. You shift from Construction to Cultivation. You shift from the heavy lifting of *Building* to the quiet, rhythmic work of *Tending*.

Tending is different. Tending is walking out into your yard with a cup of coffee in the morning and noticing, *Oh, there's a weed growing by the rosebush.* You bend down, pull it out, and keep walking.

You don't shutdown. You don't collapse and think, *"I FAILED! THERE IS A WEED! TEAR DOWN THE HOUSE!"*

You just tend to it.

Living a life of healthy boundaries is simply the daily practice of Tending. It is the small, undramatic adjustments you make as you go.

Some days, you will notice a weed of resentment growing because you said "yes" too quickly. You simply pluck it out by canceling the plan or adjusting your attitude.

Some seasons, a storm will come, a family crisis, a health scare, a new baby, and a section of your fence might blow down. That isn't a moral failure. It's just weather. You wait for the storm to pass, and then you go out, pick up the hammer, and repair that section.

You do it without shame. You do it without the frantic "I'm off the wagon" narrative. You do it because you are the Gardener, and this is your land to keep.

UNDERSTANDING YOUR SEASONS

Part of being a good gardener is respecting the seasons.

In our "super-Christian-super-woman" culture, we expect ourselves to be in a perpetual Summer Harvest. We think we should always be producing, always helpful, always energetic, and always perfectly boundaried.

But nature doesn't work that way, and neither do you.

There will be Winter Seasons. These are times of grief, illness, postpartum, or deep transition. In a Winter Season, your capacity is low. Your only job is to keep the gate locked and the fire burning inside. You might not have the energy for "Kind Honesty" scripts or gentle explanations. You might just need to say "No" and go to sleep. That is not failure; that is dormancy. It is how you survive to see the Spring.

There will be Spring Seasons. You have new energy. You might feel ready to tackle a hard conversation with your mother-in-law or re-negotiate a role at work. You feel growth happening. It's messy and muddy, but it's alive.

There will be Summer Seasons. The fruit is abundant. You have energy to give! You can say "Yes" to the meal train, the volunteer role, and the late-night phone call because your tank is full. Enjoy this. Pour out from your overflow.

And there will be Fall Seasons. You sense the capacity shifting. You start to pull back. You start to harvest what you've grown and prepare for rest.

If you try to act like it's Summer when you are physically and emotionally in Winter, you will break. Secure love means looking at the season you are actually in, not the season you wish you were in, and stewarding it with grace.

The Art of Pruning (And The Grief That Follows)

There is one part of gardening we haven't talked about yet, and honestly, it is the hardest part. It is the part that makes most of us want to throw down our shears and run back to the safety of people-pleasing.

Pruning.

Sometimes, tending a garden doesn't just mean watering the flowers; it means cutting back the dead weight. It means looking at a branch that is sucking the life out of the tree, maybe a relationship that is entirely one-sided, or a commitment that used to give you joy but now only brings dread, and cutting it back.

To the untrained eye, pruning looks like destruction. It looks like you are hurting the plant. But the gardener knows the truth: *We prune so that life can flourish.*

As you continue this reset, you may discover that some relationships in your life cannot survive your boundaries. When you stop over-functioning, some people may stop calling. When you stop playing the role of the "Fixer," some friends may drift away because there is nothing left for you to fix.

This is painful. It brings up a very specific type of grief. You might think, *"If I were doing this right, everyone would be happy."*

But Jesus tells us in John 15 that every branch that bears fruit is pruned so that it will be *even more fruitful*. If you are in a season of pruning, if your circle is getting smaller, if some people are falling away because they only loved you for your utility, not your soul, do not panic.

You are not losing; you are concentrating your energy. You are removing the invasive species so that the real fruit, the relationships that are reciprocal, safe, and honoring, can finally breathe. Let yourself grieve the loss, but trust the Gardener. He knows what He is doing.

THE "CLUNKY PHASE" (WHY YOU FEEL LIKE A ROBOT)

Another fear I hear constantly is this: *"I feel so fake. When I use these scripts, I sound like a robot. I miss the old me who just flowed naturally."*

I want to validate that. Yes, you feel robotic right now. That is actually a sign that you are learning.

In psychology, the "Four Stages of Competence" explains exactly what is happening in your brain right now.

Stage 1: Unconscious Incompetence. This was you before you picked up this book. You were over-functioning and resentful, but you didn't realize a lack of boundaries was the problem. You just thought you were tired.

Stage 2: Conscious Incompetence (The "Ouch" Phase). This is when you wake up. You realize, *Oh no. I have no boundaries.* This stage is painful. You see the problem, but you don't have the skills to fix it yet.

Stage 3: Conscious Competence (The "Robot" Phase). This is where you likely are right now. You have the skills, the scripts, the pause, the check-in, but you have to think about them really hard. You have to rehearse the line in the bathroom mirror. You have to check your notes before you send the text. It feels clunky. It feels mechanical. But please, do not stop here. Do not mistake "clunky" for "fake." You are building new neural pathways. You are learning a new language. You have to speak it with an accent before you can speak it fluently.

Stage 4: Unconscious Competence (The "Flow" Phase). This is where we are heading. One day, six months from now, someone will ask you to do something you don't have time for. And without thinking, without sweating, without rehearsing, you will simply say, "I'd love to, but I can't make that work." And you will move on. It will be natural. But you need the scripts now to get you to then. Be willing to be a robot for a little while so you can be a healthy human for a lifetime.

WHEN THE OLD "YOU" SHOWS UP (THE SLIDE)

I want to normalize something that is going to happen to you. In fact, it might happen next week.

You are going to slide back.

You are going to find yourself in a situation, maybe you're back in your childhood home for a holiday, or you're exhausted from work, and suddenly, the "New You" with all her shiny boundaries will vanish.

The "Old You" will take the wheel.

You will find yourself apologizing for things you didn't do. You will find yourself laughing nervously when someone insults you. You will say "Yes" to the bake sale when you wanted to scream "No."

And afterward, the shame will try to eat you alive. *I wrote a whole book on this,* you'll think. *I read the scripts. And here I am, acting like a doormat again. I'm a fraud.*

Please hear me: You are not a fraud. You are a human being with a nervous system that prioritizes survival.

When we are stressed, tired, or in an environment that triggers our oldest wounds, our brain defaults to the path of least resistance. For you, that path is People-Pleasing. It is a well-worn superhighway in your brain, paved over decades of use.

Your new boundaries are a dirt path you have just started hacking through the jungle.

Of course, you took the highway when you were tired! It's paved!

This slide is not a failure of character; it is a failure of energy. And it is valuable data. Instead of shaming yourself, I want you to get curious. When you slide back into old habits, ask yourself:

- *What was the trigger? (Was I hungry? Tired? In a specific room?)*
- *What was I trying to protect?*
- *How can I be kind to myself right now?*

Progress is not a straight line up the mountain. It is a spiral. You might pass the same scenery again, the same conflict, the same guilt trip, but you are passing it at a higher elevation. You have more tools now.

You might still fall, but you won't stay down as long.

THE NEW METRIC: THE QUICK RETURN

This brings us to the most important shift in how we measure success.

If your definition of success is "I will never feel guilty again" or "I will never over-commit again," you are setting yourself up to lose.

The goal of the Healthy Boundaries Reset is not perfection. The goal is the **Quick Return**.

In neuroscience, there is a concept called the "Refractory Period." This is the amount of time it takes for your body to recover after an emotional reaction.

In the old days, if you set a boundary and someone got mad, you might have spiraled for three weeks. You would have lost sleep, obsessed over every text message, and eventually caved just to stop the pain. Your refractory period was twenty-one days.

Now, let's say you set a boundary today. You say "No" to a friend. She gets cold.

You feel the dread. You feel the heavy pit in your stomach. (That's the biology; it's still there).

But this time, you use the tools. You call a safe friend. You pray. You remind yourself of The Gatekeeper's Truth: *Disappointment is not harm.*

And instead of spiraling for three weeks, you spiral for three hours. By dinner time, you are breathing again. You are present with your family.

That is the victory.

You didn't avoid the feelings, but you recovered from them. You returned to peace faster. Eventually, that three hours will turn into three minutes.

Give yourself permission to be a beginner. Give yourself credit for the hours you didn't spend spiraling. That is the Holy Spirit working in you, restoring your soul, minute by minute.

The Generational Garden

Before we move to our final practices, I want you to lift your eyes from the soil for a moment and look at who is watching you garden.

For many of you, this work feels selfish. You still have that nagging voice saying, *"I'm just focusing on me, me, me."*

But you are not just gardening for yourself. You are planting seeds for the next generation.

If you have children, or if you mentor younger women, or if you are an aunt or a leader, they are watching you. They are not listening to your lectures about self-care; they are watching your life.

When they see you say a polite "No" without agonizing guilt, they learn that their own "No" is valid. When they see you rest without apologizing, they learn that worth is not tied to exhaustion. When they see you admit, "I made a mistake, let me fix it," they learn that perfection is not the price of admission for love.

You are breaking a generational curse of codependency. You are interrupting a lineage of women who were taught to set themselves on fire to keep everyone else warm. You are modeling a new way, a way where a woman can be both powerful and kind, both protected and open.

This is the legacy of the Healthy Boundaries Reset. You are not just building a fence; you are building a sanctuary for your children's children.

FROM PROTECTION TO CONNECTION

Why have we done all this work?

Why have we risked relationships, endured guilt hangovers, and learned to speak a new language? Was it just to be left alone? Was it just to sit in a fortress of solitude where no one can bother us?

No. As we said in Chapter 7, we did not build a wall; we installed a Gate.

We did this work so that we could finally, truly Love.

You cannot love someone you are terrified of. You cannot love someone you are secretly resenting. You cannot love someone if you are disappearing to keep them happy.

Now that you have your "Separate Self," you are capable of true intimacy. Because you are safe, you can now afford to be soft.

This is where the journey goes next. In the first book, *Anxious Attachment Reset*, we learned how to find safety within ourselves and God. In this book, we learned how to create safety with others through limits.

Now, the invitation is to use that safety to build deep, rich, vulnerable connection.

Now that you know how to say "No," your "Yes" is powerful. Now that you know how to protect your yard, you can invite people in for a garden party.

But for now, look around your garden.

Look at the space you have created. It is quiet. It is peaceful. It is yours.

You are no longer a slave to the urgent. You are a daughter of the King, and you have learned to steward your inheritance.

THE BOUNDARY BUILDER: DAILY PRACTICES

Maintenance doesn't have to be heavy. To keep your garden growing, you don't need a chainsaw; you just need a watering can. Here are five gentle, low-pressure practices to help you maintain your reset in the months to come.

1. **The Morning Capacity Check:** Before you look at your phone, before you check your email, before you ask your family what they need, ask yourself: *What is in my tank today? Am I running on a full tank? Half? Fumes?* If you are on fumes, your boundary for the day is: "Low Output." You cancel the optional. You order pizza. You go to bed early. Honoring your capacity is the first step of stewardship.

2. **The "Let Me Check" Pause:** Keep this tool in your pocket forever. Never give an answer in the room. When asked for a favor, a volunteer role, or a commitment, your default answer is always: *"I need to check my calendar/capacity. I'll let you know tomorrow."* This single habit will save you from 90% of your resentment.

3. **The Phone Sabbatical:** Your phone is the primary way the world breaches your boundaries. Choose a time, maybe from 8:00 PM to 8:00 AM, or maybe all day Sunday, where the gate is locked. Use "Do Not Disturb" mode. Let the texts pile up. Reclaim the right to be unreachable.

4. **The "No" Audit:** Once a week, look back at your week and ask: *Where did I say a 'Resentful Yes'?* Don't judge it. Just notice

it. "Oh, I said yes to that coffee date because I felt guilty." Next time, try a "Kind No."

5. **The Exhale Prayer:** When you feel the tightness of anxiety, the pressure to fix, or the urge to rescue, stop. Physically stop moving. Inhale deeply and say: *"I am responsible to them."* Exhale slowly and say: *"I am not responsible for them."* Repeat until your shoulders drop.

BENEDICTION: A PRAYER FOR THE GATEKEEPER

As we close this book, I want to pray a blessing over you, the Gatekeeper of your own heart.

Lord,

We thank You that You are a God of order, not chaos. We thank You that You set boundaries, separating the light from the dark, the sea from the land, so that life could flourish.

I pray for my friend reading these words.

Give her the courage to hold her lines when her hands are shaking. Give her the wisdom to know the difference between a need she can meet and a burden she must release.

When she feels the weight of guilt, remind her that she is not the Savior. You are. When she feels the fear of rejection, remind her that she is already chosen, already held, and already approved by You.

Bless her "No," that it may protect her peace. Bless her "Yes," that it may be full of joy.

And may her life be a garden, watered, tended, and safe, where Your love can grow in abundance.

In the name of Jesus, who withdrew to the mountains to pray and came back to save the world,

Amen.

You are ready.

You have the tools. You have the permission. You have the Gate.

Open it when you choose. Close it

Based on the draft of "Healthy Boundaries Reset," here is a **References** section tailored to match the tone, style, and content of your previous book's back matter. I have updated the citations to reflect the specific concepts (Family Systems, the "Fawn" response, Stewardship) and scriptures used in this specific manuscript.

THE BOUNDARY SCRIPT VAULT

(Your "Break Glass in Case of Emergency" Kit)

We have talked a lot about the *theory* of boundaries. We've talked about the theology of the Gate and the psychology of the Shock Collar. But I know that when you are standing in front of your pushy aunt or staring at a text from a demanding boss, your brain can go offline.

The "Appeasement Reflex" kicks in. Your throat tightens. And suddenly, you can't remember a single eloquent thing you read in Chapter 4.

That is what this Vault is for.

Think of this appendix as your menu. You don't have to cook the meal from scratch; you just have to order off the menu. I have organized these scripts by "Heat Level", from the gentle decline for a safe friend to the hard limit for an unsafe situation.

The Golden Rule of Scripts: You do not need to memorize these word-for-word. Adapt them to your voice. But do not add extra words just to soften the blow. When we over-talk, we dilute the truth. Say what you mean, then stop.

Level 1: The Gentle No

Use when: You are dealing with safe people who respect you, but you simply don't have the capacity (or the desire) to say yes. The goal here is to protect the relationship while protecting your time.

The "Sandwich" No: *"I love that you thought of me for this (Slice 1: Affirmation), but I'm at capacity right now and won't be able to help (The Meat: The No). I hope you find the perfect person for it! (Slice 2: Well Wishes)."*

The "Capacity Check": *"I would love to see you, but I've had a heavy week, and I need to prioritize rest this weekend, so I'm not a zombie on Monday. Can we look at next month?"*

The "Values" Decline: *"That sounds like a wonderful event. I'm focusing all my volunteer energy on [specific ministry/family] in this season, so I'm going to pass. Thank you for asking!"*

The "Soft Close" (For the dinner party invite) *"Thank you for the invite! We aren't able to make it, but I hope you guys have the best time."* (Note: Notice I didn't say **why** we can't make it. You don't owe an explanation for your absence).

Level 2: The Firm No

Use when: The person is pushy, guilt-inducing, or has a history of not hearing your "soft" no. This requires you to remove the "JADE" (Justify, Argue, Defend, Explain).

The "No JADE" Statement: *"I'm not able to help with that."* (If they ask why: *"It just doesn't work for my schedule."*)

The "Policy" Approach (Great for work or business): *"I have a personal policy that I don't check email after 6:00 PM / I don't lend money to friends. I value our relationship too much to blur those lines."*

The "Partial Yes" (The Gatekeeper's Compromise): *"I can't take on the whole project, but I can give you fifteen minutes to brainstorm a direction. After that, I'll need to step back."*

The **"Resentment Prevention" Script:** *"I realized that if I said 'yes' to this, I would feel rushed and resentful, and I care about you too much to bring that energy into our relationship. So I'm going to say no."*

Level 3: The Broken Record

Use when: You have set a boundary, and they are arguing, negotiating, or guilt-tripping. Do not engage with the content of their argument. Simply repeat your limit.

The Scenario: Your mother wants you to come for Christmas, but you have decided to stay home.

- **Mom:** "But you always come! Dad will be so sad."
- **You:** "I know it's disappointing. We love you, but we are staying home this year."
- **Mom:** "That is so selfish. We won't be around forever."
- **You:** "I hear that you're hurt, and I'm sorry this is hard. But we are staying home this year."
- **Mom:** "So you don't care about us?"
- **You:** "I love you deeply. And we are staying home this year."

(See what happened? You didn't take the bait. You didn't explain. You stood at the Gate and didn't move.)

Level 4: The Exit Strategy (Toxic/Unsafe)

Use when: The interaction has become abusive, aggressive, or cyclical. You are no longer negotiating; you are evacuating.

The "Stop" Sign: *"I'm not willing to be spoken to this way. I'm going to hang up/leave now."*

The "Pause for Safety": *"This conversation is no longer productive. I'm going to step away. We can try again when we are both calm."*

The "Topic Shutdown" (For intrusive questions): *"I'm not going to discuss my weight/marriage/finances with you. Please stop asking."* (If they ask again: *"I asked you to stop. Since you haven't, I'm leaving."*)

Level 5: The "Buy Time" Scripts (The Pause)

Use when: You feel the pressure to answer *now*, and your "Appeasement Reflex" is about to scream "YES!" Use these to unplug the shock collar.

The "Let Me Check": *"I need to check my calendar/budget before I commit to anything. I'll get back to you on Tuesday."*

The "Spouse Buffer": *"We've made a rule that we don't say yes to anything without discussing it together first. I'll let you know."*

The "24-Hour Rule": *"I make it a practice to take 24 hours before adding anything new to my plate. I'll text you tomorrow."*

Level 6: The Digital Gatekeeper

Use when: The phone is buzzing, and you feel the phantom urgency of the digital world.

The "Auto-Reply" (For your personal life): *"Hey! I'm taking a break from my phone this weekend to be present with my family. I'll get back to you next week!"*

The "Slow Reply" Expectation: *"I saw this and want to give it my full attention, but I'm swamped right now. I'll reply properly in a day or two!"*

The "Group Chat" Exit: *"Hey everyone! I need to clear some digital clutter for my mental health, so I'm hopping off this thread. Love you guys!"*

A Final Note: The Script is Just the Wrapper

Remember, the words matter, but the **posture** matters more.

If you say these scripts while trembling, apologizing, and looking at the floor, the other person will sense your hesitation. They will rattle the gate.

Before you speak, ground yourself.

1. **Feet flat on the floor.** (Physical stability).
2. **Deep breath.** (Nervous system regulation).
3. **Remember the Truth:** *"I am allowed to have limits. My 'No' protects my 'Yes.'"*

You are not being mean. You are being clear. And as Brené Brown says, "Clear is kind."

Go use your voice. You've got this.

REFERENCES

Or: The Receipts That Prove I Didn't Just Make Up "The Fawn Response"

Okay, I know. You just finished a book about learning to say "No," and the last thing you want to do is say "Yes" to reading a bibliography. But here is the thing: the concepts in this book, from the "Change Back Maneuver" to the "Fawn Response", aren't just my personal opinions. They are backed by decades of research into how families work, how trauma affects the body, and how God designed the human soul.

Consider this section the structural beams behind the drywall. You don't always see them, but they are holding the whole house up.

BOOKS AND ACADEMIC SOURCES

Cloud, H., & Townsend, J. (1992). *Boundaries: When to Say Yes, How to Say No to Take Control of Your Life.* **Zondervan.** The absolute gold standard. If you haven't read this, go buy it immediately. It's the textbook for everything we talked about regarding stewardship and responsibility.

Lerner, H. (1985). *The Dance of Anger: A Woman's Guide to Changing the Patterns of Intimate Relationships.* **Harper & Row.** Dr. Lerner is the one who popularized the concept of the "Change Back" maneuver (she calls it "Countermoves"). Essential reading if you want to understand why your family loses their minds when you change your steps.

Walker, P. (2013). *Complex PTSD: From Surviving to Thriving.* **Azure Coyote.** This is where we get the deep dive into the "Fawn" response (the people-pleasing trauma response) alongside Fight, Flight, and Freeze. If you identified heavily with the "Appeasement Reflex," this work is vital.

Brown, B. (2018). *Dare to Lead: Brave Work. Tough Conversations. Whole Hearts.* **Random House.** The source of the life-changing mantra "Clear is Kind. Unclear is Unkind." Brené Brown's work on vulnerability is the antidote to the "Nice Girl" syndrome.

Friedman, E. H. (1985). *Generation to Generation: Family Process in Church and Synagogue.* **Guilford Press.** A heavy hitter on Family Systems Theory. This explains why one person setting a boundary disrupts the whole mobile (the system), and why leaders (and parents) often face sabotage when they get healthy.

SCRIPTURE REFERENCES

Because God was the first one to draw a line in the sand.

All Scripture quotations are taken from the New International Version® (NIV®). Copyright ©1973, 1978, 1984, 2011 by Biblica, Inc.™ Used by permission. All rights reserved worldwide.

Old Testament References: (Where we learn that boundaries create order out of chaos)

- **Genesis 1:3-4**, "God saw that the light was good, and he separated the light from the darkness." (The first boundary).
- **Genesis 2:24** "That is why a man leaves his father and mother and is united to his wife, and they become one flesh." (The "Leave and Cleave" boundary).
- **1 Samuel 24:22**, "Then Saul went home, but David and his men went up to the stronghold." (David's boundary: Forgiveness without proximity).
- **Job 38:11** "This far you may come and no farther; here is where your proud waves halt."
- **Psalm 16:6**, "The boundary lines have fallen for me in pleasant places; surely I have a delightful inheritance."
- **Psalm 127:2**, "In vain you rise early and stay up late, toiling for food to eat, for he grants sleep to those he loves."
- **Proverbs 4:23**, "Above all else, guard your heart, for everything you do flows from it." (The Gatekeeper verse).
- **Proverbs 25:28**, "Like a city whose walls are broken through is a person who lacks self-control."
- **Proverbs 27:6**, "Faithful are the wounds of a friend; profuse are the kisses of an enemy."

New Testament References: (Where Jesus models how to disappoint people to stay on mission)

- **Matthew 5:9**, "Blessed are the peacemakers, for they will be called children of God."
- **Matthew 5:37**, "All you need to say is simply 'Yes' or 'No'; anything beyond this comes from the evil one."
- **Matthew 7:16**, "By their fruit you will recognize them." (The Fruit Inspection).
- **Matthew 10:34**, "Do not suppose that I have come to bring peace to the earth. I did not come to bring peace, but a sword."
- **Mark 1:35-38**, Jesus leaves the needy crowd in Capernaum to preach elsewhere. (The "No" to the good to say "Yes" to the best).
- **Mark 4:38**, "Jesus was in the stern, sleeping on a cushion." (The boundary of rest).
- **Luke 5:16**, "But Jesus often withdrew to lonely places and prayed."
- **John 2:24**, "But Jesus would not entrust himself to them, for he knew all people." (Forgiveness vs. Trust).

- **John 11:5-6**, "Now Jesus loved Martha and her sister and Lazarus. So when he heard that Lazarus was sick, he stayed where he was two more days." (The Lazarus Boundary).
- **Galatians 6:2, 5**, "Carry each other's burdens... for each one should carry their own load." (The Knapsack vs. The Boulder).
- **Ephesians 4:25**, "Therefore each of you must put off falsehood and speak truthfully to your neighbor."

AUTHOR'S NOTE

Or: Why I Use Psychology and Jesus in the Same Sentence

This book is a hybrid creature. It integrates clinical insights from psychology (like family systems theory and trauma responses) with the eternal truth of Scripture. I operate under the conviction that all truth is God's truth. Whether we learn about the nervous system from a neuroscientist or about the soul from an apostle, we are learning about the intricate design of our Creator.

The psychological tools provided here (scripts, nervous system regulation, cognitive reframing) are mechanisms to help us live out the biblical commands to love well, speak truth, and steward our lives.

FOR FURTHER READING

Or: Books That Will Help You Keep the Gate Locked When You Want to Cave

If you want to go deeper into specific areas we touched on, like codependency, difficult conversations, or theology, here is your reading list.

The Classics on Boundaries:

- *Boundaries* by Dr. Henry Cloud & Dr. John Townsend (The manual).
- *Good Boundaries and Goodbyes* by Lysa TerKeurst (A fantastic theological look at why access requires responsibility).

On Breaking Codependency:

- *Codependent No More* by Melody Beattie (The book that defined the "Fixer" role).
- *The Best Yes* by Lysa TerKeurst (Great for the "over-committed" woman).

On Communication and Conflict:

- *Crucial Conversations* by Kerry Patterson et al. (Advanced scripts for high-stakes talks).
- *The Peacemaker* by Ken Sande (Biblical conflict resolution that distinguishes between peace-faking and peace-making).

PROFESSIONAL RESOURCES

This book is a guide, not a clinician. If you are in a relationship involving physical abuse, severe narcissism, or safety threats, a book is not enough protection. Please seek professional help. The American Association of Christian Counselors (aacc.net) is a great place to find a therapist who understands both your mental health and your faith.

Remember: You are worth protecting. The gate is yours to keep.